Blockchain

———— ✺❧✺❧✺ ————

Understanding the Blockchain Revolution and the Technology Behind It

Mark Smith

Introduction

I want to thank you and congratulate you for purchasing the book, *"Blockchain: Understanding the Blockchain Revolution and the Technology Behind It"*.

This book contains proven steps and strategies on how to understand fully what a blockchain is, what the revolution is all about and the technology that is behind it all, driving one of the biggest innovations in IT for many years.

You will learn what a blockchain is, and then what the blockchain technology is. I will talk about how blockchain technology is going to change the world we live in irrevocably and forever.

Many of you have probably heard the term, "blockchain", many times over the last few years. That's because it is the technology that underpins the Bitcoin, the digital currency that more and more people are turning to. Banks believe that the blockchain could become the future of all financial transactions and governments are being strongly urged to adopt the technology as a permanent and tamper-free way of storing data and transactions.

Now I'm going to take you into the world of blockchain, the technology that drives it and what it means for us in the future.

Thanks again for purchasing this book, I hope you enjoy it!

The information herein is offered for informational purposes solely, and is universal as so. The presentation of the information is without contract or any type of guarantee assurance.

The trademarks that are used are without any consent, and the publication of the trademark is without permission or backing by the trademark owner. All trademarks and brands within this book are for clarifying purposes only and are the owned by the owners themselves, not affiliated with this document.

Table of Contents

Part 1:

Understanding the Blockchain and the Technology Behind it

Chapter 1:
What is a Blockchain?

A blockchain is a database that holds a series of records in a list that is ever expanding. Each record is called a block and the blockchain is fully secured from any form of tampering and from revision. Each of the records, or blocks, is time stamped and is also linked to the record before it, hence the chain.

We all know of blockchains as being the underlying technology of the virtual currency, the bitcoin. The idea of the bitcoin was born in 2008 and in 2009 it became a reality and the blockchain is actually a public ledger of every bitcoin transaction. In the case of the bitcoin, each client can connect to the network and can send transactions to the network. They can also verify transactions, and take part in the heavy competition to make new blocks, a competition known as mining.

A Brief History

When it was first thought of, the blockchain really was only for the bitcoin and was derived as the answer to making databases completely secure and with the ability to be distributed widely. From 2014, the term "blockchain 2.0" began to be used in the database field and this second-generation blockchain was described by The Economist as having a "programmable language that allows users to write more sophisticated smart contracts, thus creating invoices that pay themselves when a shipment arrives or shares certificates which automatically send their owners dividends if profits reach a certain level".

In 2016, a pilot project based on blockchain technology was announced by the central securities depository of the Russian Federations and a number of music industry regulatory bodies have begun to test out models for the collection of royalties and copyright management using blockchain technology.

How a Blockchain is Formed

Each blockchain is made up of blocks, each of which holds a valid transaction. Each of the blocks will include a hash of the block before it and this is what links the two together. These links form the chain. As well as containing a hash-based history, every blockchain database will also contain a specific algorithm. This is used to score different versions of the histories and this enables one version of a higher value to be chosen above the others. Peers that support the blockchain databases do not have access to the same versions of the history all of the time, instead, they just hang onto the version that scores the highest (at least that they know of). When a peer gets a newer version with a higher score, it will normally be the one they already have with a new block added to the chain. At this point, they will overwrite the database that they hold and then send the improvement to the other peers. However, there is absolutely no guarantee that one entry will stay in the highest scoring database version forever but, as a blockchain is built to add on the score of a new block to the total score of the existing blocks, there is a low probability of an entry being superseded, especially as more blocks go on and because there are certain incentives to working in adding new blocks to extend, rather than working just with old blocks.

Decentralization

By the very fact that a blockchain stores data across the network, it cuts out the risks that always go with centrally held data. This is because the network does not have the centralized points that are vulnerable, and this means hackers cannot exploit them. We all know that the internet has a ton of security problems today; how many of us still rely on the system of usernames and passwords to protect data and identity and these are easily hacked whereas the blockchain uses encryption technology for security.

Encryption technology is based on a system of private and public keys. The public key is a long string of numbers, generated randomly and this is the blockchain address of the user. The transaction that goes across the network is recorded on that key and is down as belonging to that specific user. The private key, on the other hand, is similar to a password and it is what allows the owner access to their digital assets. If you store data on a blockchain, it cannot be corrupted but you will need to take some extra measures – you need to create a paper wallet, and print your private key to safeguard it.

Blockchain

Every single node that is contained in a decentralized system contains a copy of the blockchain. There is no official centralized copy anywhere and no one user is given any more trust than another. All transactions are sent to the network through the use of the software. Mining nodes are then used to validate each of the transactions and then add them to the blockchain that is being created. The entire block is then sent to the other nodes. Each change is serialized through the use of timestamps.

In the beginning, blockchains used to be permission less and this has led to a certain amount of controversy over whether a permissioned database containing chained data blocks should actually be known as a blockchain. This is an ongoing debate and the crux of it is whether private systems that have verifiers who are tasked by and authorized by a central authority should actually be a blockchain.

Those in favor of private chains say that the term, "blockchain" should be applied to all data structures that put batches of time stamped data because the blockchains are a distributed version of MVCC (multi version concurrency). MVCC will not allow two transactions to concurrently make any modifications to an object within a database and, in the same way, blockchains also stop two transactions from spending a single output within a blockchain.

Opponents say that a permissioned blockchain looks very much like a traditional database and doesn't support decentralized data verification. These systems are not safe from tampering and are not secure from being revised by the operators. According to the Harvard Business Review, a blockchain is a "distributed ledger or database that is open to anyone" and Computerworld says that most of the hype that surrounds blockchains is nothing more than "snake oil and spin".

Applications

The blockchain technology, which I will talk about in more detail later on, can be integrated into several areas, including digital currency, payment systems, crowd sale facilitations, implementation of prediction markets and generic tools for governance. Major blockchain applications include:

Cryptocurrency:

- Bitcoin

- Ripple

- BlackCoin

- Nxt

- Dash

Blockchain Platforms:

- Factom – distributed registry

- MainSafe – software for decentralized applications

- Gems – decentralized messaging

- Stori – distributed cloud

- Tezos – decentralized voting

Applications

According to a research project carried out over 2 years by the Harvard business review, blockchain technology can be used to store and host, in a secure environment:

- Money

- Titles

- Deeds

- Music

- Art

- Intellectual property

- Scientific discoveries

- Votes

Chapter 2:
Understanding the Blockchain Technology

There is absolutely no doubt that the focus that was once on the single cryptocurrency (bitcoin) is fast moving towards applications that are based on cryptocurrency and built on the blockchain. The technology behind a blockchain is pretty much the same as that in a database but with one exception – the way that we interact with them is different.

For a developer, the concept of the blockchain is a radical change in the way that software applications of the future will be written. It is a key concept that has to be thoroughly understood, along with the other 4 of the 5 main concepts. We also need to understand how the concepts interrelate in the context of the blockchain technology. Those key concepts are:

1. The blockchain itself

2. The decentralized consensus

3. Trusted computing

4. Smart contracts

5. Proof of work

This paradigm is very important because it is the drive behind the creation of the decentralized application, the next step up in the evolution of the architectural constructs of distributed computing.

But this is by no means only a computing wonder. Applications that have been decentralized are going to be able to enable a trend of decentralization at 4 levels – business, governance, legal and societal. This is because the race is on to make everything decentralized and put the power at the edge of the networks. Let's take a look at each of these concepts in more detail:

1. **The Blockchain and the Blockchain Services**

A blockchain is a place where data is stored semi publicly in a block. Anyone can see who verified the block because it will have a signature on it but the only ones who can actually unlock the data inside the block are you or a specified program. This is because only the owner of the data has the private key to unlock it.

So, a blockchain is pretty much like a database with the exception that the header, or part of the stored information, is actually public. Stored data can be a balance of cryptocurrency or a toke of some value. In essence, the blockchain is an alternative system for value transfer, one that can be tampered with by malicious third parties or accessed by centralized agencies. The encryption is based on public and private keys – public visibility but only for private inspection. Your home address could be publicly advertised but it wouldn't give any information about how to get in your home or what it is like inside. That can only be done through a private key and, as that address has been claimed as yours, no one else can claim it.

The blockchain is also a software approach that binds several peer computers together, all of which will obey the consensus process of the release of information or for recording what information is held and is also where every interaction is cryptographically verified.

2. **The Decentralized Consensus**

This breaks the existing model of the centralized consensus, for example, when a central database was used to rule over the validity of transactions. Decentralized schemes, which the blockchain is based on, transfer the authority and the trust over to a virtual network that has been decentralized, thus allowing the nodes to record all transactions, on a continuous basis and in sequence, on public blocks, thus creating the chain. Each block contains a fingerprint, or a hash, of the block before it. Cryptography is used as a way of securing the authentication of each source though the use of these hashes and that eliminates the requirement or the need for any centralized intermediately. The combination of the blockchain technology and the cryptography ensures that no transaction is ever recorded in duplicate.

There is an important factor in this unbundling – the consensus logic is kept separated from the application, which means that the application can be specifically written to be decentralized. That is the dynamite that is needed to kick off a whole series of system-changing innovations within the application software architecture, whether they are related to money or not.

3. **Trusted Computing**

Or, as some call it, trustless transactions. When you put together the concepts that are behind the blockchain – the smart contracts and the decentralized consensus – you begin to see that they are actually helping transactions and resources to spread in a lateral peer-to-peer manner and, in doing so, they are also enabling the computer to have trust in one another at a very deep level.

Where central organizations and institutions are seen as necessary to be trusted authorities, some of the centralized functions can actually be codified in a smart contract that is under the governance of a decentralized consensus on the blockchain.

Because the blockchain has the role of validating transactions, each of the peers can go head and trust each other because living on the technology are a number of rules:

- Trust

- Compliance

- Governance

- Authority

- Contracts

- Law

- Agreements

If you look ahead to the future, not too far ahead, smart property and smart contracts will be automatically created and executed between parties without either knowing that the blockchain was even involved as the trusted intermediary.

4. **Smart Contracts**

These are building blocks for the decentralized application. Smart contracts are like small programs that you can give a unit of value to, whether it is money or a token, along with the rules that govern that value. The idea behind the smart contract is so that any contractual governance between at least two parties for each transaction can be verified via the blockchain. There is no need to have a centralized agency when the parties can come to an agreement between them and when they can put the terms and the implications of the agreement directly into the program. Those terms include the fulfillment of services sequentially and penalties if a transaction is not fulfilled.

When you apply a smart contract, you assume that there is no need for a third-party intermediary to conduct any transaction between two or more parties. Instead, the parties will come to an agreement between them on the definition of the rules and ensure that they are embedded within the transaction. This means that the end-to-end resolution is self-managed between the computers that are representing the user interest. A smart property is a digital asset that knows exactly who its owner is and the ownership is generally linked into the blockchain.

5. **Proof of Work**

At the very heart of the operations in a blockchain is this concept. Proof of work was an important part of the original blockchain role as the transaction authenticator. Proof of work is what provides the right to take part in the blockchain and it is displayed as a large hurdle that stops users from making changes to records stored on the chain without providing a new proof of work.

It is one of the main building blocks simply because it can never be undone and is cryptographically secured through the hashes that are used to prove its authenticity. However, it an expensive concept to maintain, estimated to cost about $600 million a year jut for bitcoin and that means there could be future issues of scalability and security. This is because it depends entirely on the incentives for the miners – mining will decline as time goes by. A better solution is called "proof of stake" – much cheaper for enforcing but way more expensive and much more difficult to compromise. This concept will determine who is allowed to update the consensus and stop the underlying blockchain from being forked.

Moving Towards Decentralization

In the near future, we will be facing a rush to come up with decentralized applications that enable the new decentralized world we are fast heading for. Because of that, both visionaries and business leaders will have to learn a brand new vocabulary that based on crypto frameworks. Developers are going to have to learn how to write these decentralized apps that will be enabled by the technology behind the blockchain. And the end-user has to learn all about the smart contract, how to create them and how to use them. Developmental environments will need to be comprehensive and will need to support a whole range of capabilities and components on the blockchain services and on the consensus engine.

Blockchain technology for the bitcoin had a number of limitations that came to light as we began to push it outside of services that were related to money and into the realms of software applications. We really shouldn't be surprised that multiple blockchains as the way forward and some of them will work together, others will compete against one another while yet others will simply be benevolent.

These decentralized apps will be all different sizes, different flavors and the whole range of complexity levels so we have to be fully prepared for all of the variety. We have to be able to see beyond what the bitcoin promised and right into the heart of the blockchain promise to become the brand new environment development, in the same way that, back in 1996, web development was the environment.

That said, decentralized applications cannot be used for everything and we will find that some things simply won't fit into the paradigm of the decentralized application. There are a number of applications that do fit the bill and that gives us a nice number of opportunities or visionaries, creators, and developers to take advantage of. We will call them blockchain apps for now.

Emerging Blockchain Application Segments

There are four of these and I will discuss each one in turn:

- Currency

- Pegged Services

- Smart Contracts

- Distributed Autonomous Organization

Currency

This segment is aimed at payments, monetary transfers, tips, and funding applications. The end users will either use an exchange or their own wallet for these types of transactions and they reap the benefits of reductions in the transaction costs, a speedy settlement and not having to go through a centralized agency. Today, exchanges have been centralized but we are likely to see a future generation of trusted exchanges that are decentralized. Although the wallets used for bitcoin are classed as "dumb", future wallets are likely to become smarter with the ability to launch a smart contract.

Pegged Services

This is a rather interesting segment. Services that are pegged to the blockchain are able to make use of the atomic unit in the chain. This is a capability that stores values but the pegged service can also build on that with their own off-chain services. An example of this would be a decentralized ownership or agency, which is horizontal service, being able to be applied to any vertical segment, such as photography, music, or videos, to name just a few.

Smart Contracts

We already know what the smart contract is but, in terms of the segment, they are representative of a simple decentralization form. They are expected to become fully available in several application areas, for example, family trusts, wagers, time stamping, escrow, proof of work, etc. In short, they are all about the movement of value or assets between owners, based on a condition or an event. They are representative of an "intermediate state" between two or more parties and we will place trust in them to verify and to take logic-based action behind the changes in the state.

Distributed Autonomous Organization

Putting aside legal issues, these are sort incorporated on the blockchain. This is because the governance of them is dependent on the end-user. The end-user is a part-users, a part owner, and part-node on the decentralized network. The key parts of a DAO are that every user is a worker and by virtue of that, they make some contribution to the appreciation of the value of the DAO through their activity or participation.

Examples of the Segment Uses

- **Currency Category** – Protocol users are payment processors, wallets, miners, and exchanges. Their frequency is sporadic and the benefits are speed and cost

- **Pegged Services Category** – Protocol users are web businesses and their frequency is chronic. Benefits are flexibility, empowered users, openness, network effects and new business models

- **Smart Contracts Category** – Protocol users are web apps, contract service providers, end-users with the use of self-service tools and their frequency is episodic. Benefits are cost, autonomy, speed and irrefutability

- **Decentralized Autonomous Organizations Category** – Protocol users are the DAO itself and the frequency is habitual. Benefits include user voice, user protection, user governance, sovereignty, self-regulation, and transparency.

There are probably more categories but these are the most important ones and the examples are purely a sample. However, for each and every segment, users should be asking themselves two questions – "what is the benefit?" and "Is there a good reason why I should participate?" The provider of the blockchain applications should focus their attention on answering these two questions in the clearest and most compelling way possible. The end-user is the fuel that fires the engine of the application success and it is, therefore, vital to stay near to the potential of the network effects on blockchain applications

Part 2:

Potential Uses for the Blockchain Technology

Chapter 3:
The Banking Industry

There are a number of different potential uses for the blockchain technology, including, with use cases:

- **Technology Decentralization**

Financial institutions and banks have been very active in investing both money and time into this area. We will now take a look at some of these institutions who are showing true interest in the blockchain:

- **Deutsche Bank**

The Deutsche bank has been investing heavily into looking at the use cases of the blockchain in the regions of fiat currency settlement, payments, enforcement, asset registries, clearing derivative contracts, KYC, improving the processing services post-trade, regulatory reporting, etc. It has run several experiments on the technology in the innovation labs in Silicon Valley, Berlin, and London

- **NASDAQ**

The NASDAQ stock exchange revealed recently that they were going to be using blockchain as a business-wide technology to improve their qualification on the Private Market Platform. This is a brand new initiative that started in 2014 and enables Pre-IPO trading between private companies. The stock exchange has also revealed that they will use the clout of the Open Assets Protocol to build up their own private platform. Later on, they then announced that they had gone into a partnership with a blockchain infrastructure called Chain, a provider specifically aimed at financial institutions and business users.

- **DBS Bank**

DBS bank was responsible for organizing and initiating a Blockchain hackathon. They did this in conjunction with Coin Republic, a bitcoin company based in Singapore. The APIs for the hackathon, which lasted for two days were provided by Blockstrap, BitX and Colu and the winners were an investment platform aimed at the emerging markets, called Omnichain. Nubank, a provider of "banking for the unbanked" came in second and BlockIntel, a transactions security platform came third.

- **EBA**

The Euro Banking Association released a report in 2015 that discussed the impact of using crypto-technology from the perspective of payment professional and transaction banking in the next three years. The report noted that the technology could be used with authority by banks to cut down their audit and governance costs, to provide a better time-to-market and much better products

- **US Federal Reserve**

The USFR is reported to be working together with IBM on the development of a new digital blockchain-based payment system

- **SCB**

According to a posting made on LinkedIn, the chief innovation officer of the Standard Chartered Bank, Anju Patwardhan, says that blockchains could be used to cut down on costs and on improving the transparency of all financial transactions.

As well as these, there are also reports that CME Group, and Deutsche Boerse, both derivatives companies, along with clearing houses EuroCPP and DTCC are all working on projects that surround using blockchain in clearing, amongst other areas. And, there has been talk of Western Union possible looking into the use of Ripple technology

Below are some of the banks that are experimenting with the use of Blockchain:

Blockchain

- **Fidor Bank**

The bank has entered a partnership with Bitcoi.de, a German peer-to-peer BTC trading Platform and with Kraken to come up with an exchange for digital currency within the EU. They also partnered up with Ripple Labs so that they could provide money transfer services

- **LHV Bank**

This bank is reported to have begun working on the blockchain technology back in 2014 and, since then, have come up with an app called Cuber Wallet, based on colored coins. They have also gone into partnership with Coinfloor and Coin base to experiment with blockchain-based digital security

- **CBW Bank and Cross River Bank**

Both have gone into partnership with Ripple Labs to come up with a risk management system and to provide remittance services at a lower cost.

- **Rabobank, ING Bank, and ABN Amro**

All are currently exploring the blockchain technology for a number of different services Rabobank has also gone into partnership with Ripple Labs

- **Goldman Sachs**

Goldman Sachs were the lead investors in Circle Internet Financial Ltd, a bitcoin startup that required initial funding of $50 million.

- **BBVA Ventures**

BBVA are Coinbase investors and have also released a report stating that they are fully interested in the use of blockchain technology

- **Santander**

Santander claims that they have at least 20-25 use cases for the blockchain technology and has set up a dedicated team called Crypto 2.0 to investigate how blockchains can be used in banking

- **Westpac**

Westpac has gone into partnership with Ripple Labs to come up with a low-cost system of cross-border payments. Its venture capital arm, called Reinventure, took part in the Series C funding venture for Coinbase.

- **UBS**

UBS has a cryptocurrency lab based in London and is currently running experiments on trading and settlement, payments and smart bonds. It has a plan to build a product called the "utility settlement coin" in a partnership with Clearmatic and they also claim to have between 20 and 25 uses in the financial sector for the blockchain

- **BNY Mellon**

BNY have come up with BK Coins, their own currency, and use it as a recognition program in the corporation. The coins can be redeemed for gifts or rewards.

Blockchain

- **Barclays Bank**

Barclays bank has 2 bitcoin labs, based in London, that are used by a number of different blockchain entrepreneurs, businesses, and coders. They have also entered into a partnership with Safello and are currently working on developing different banking services based on the blockchain. They run accelerators to give blockchain enthusiasts a bit of mentoring and give them the chance to work on specific projects with the bank and they claim to have around 45 different blockchain-based projects that they want to work on internally

- **CBA**

Has gone into partnership with Ripple Labs to come up with a blockchain-based ledger system for use in payment settlements between its own subsidiaries

- **USAA Bank**

Have created their own research team to implement a study of the bitcoin uses

- **ANZ Bank**

Have entered into a partnership with Ripple Labs to look at the uses of blockchain

- **BNP Paribas**

Are currently running experiments on how to use blockchain to make transactions faster

- **Societe Generale**

Are planning on employing staff that have expertise in blockchain, BTC, and cryptocurrency

- **Citibank**

Citibank has set up three systems that are used to deploy blockchain technology and have also developed their own form of the bitcoin, called Citicoin. This is currently being used within Citibank as a way of learning how the digital currency trading system works

Chapter 4:
Examples of Public and Private Blockchain Concepts

The Public Blockchain

Public blockchains are platforms where anyone who is on the platform can read it or write to it. They must be able to provide proof of work, though. This area has seen quite a lot of growth in activity, as the number of potential users that blockchain technology can generate is very high. On top of that, the public blockchain is considered a decentralized blockchain. Some examples of this include:

- **Ethereum** – providers of a programming language and a decentralized platform that is for helping startup contracts and also lets developers publish their distributed applications

- **Factom** – providers of records business processes and records management for governments and other businesses

- **Blockstream** – providers of a sidechain technology that is focused on extending the capabilities that bitcoin currently has. They have now begun experiments on using public blockchain technology for providing accounting, a function that was once considered to be done on the private blockchain.

Private Blockchains

Private blockchains are those that will only let the owner have the right to make changes that need to be made. This is somewhat similar to the infrastructure that already exists whereby the owner, which would be a centralized agency or authority, would have the power to revert transactions, change the rules, etc., based entirely on need. This concept is huge and could attract massive interest from financial institutions and large businesses and could, in theory, find use cases to come up with proprietary systems and cut costs while concurrently increasing efficiency. Some examples are:

- **Eris Industries** – they aim to be the only provider of shared software databases that make use of blockchain technology

- **Blockstack** - they aim to be the providers to the back office operations of financial institutions, including settlement and clearing on private blockchains

- **Multichain** – providers of a distributed database that is open source for financial transactions

- **Chain Inc.** – providers of APIs. They are chain partnered with the NAZDAQ OMX Group Inc. and provide platforms that allow the trading of private business shares using the blockchain

Hybrid Blockchain Concepts

Is there such a thing? A consortium blockchain would be a combination of a public and a private blockchain. This would mean that the ability to both read and write to it would be extended to several modes or people. This would be able to be used by companies who join forces and collaborate on the development of different models. As such, they could actually gain a blockchain that has restricted access, they could work together on their solutions and still maintain intellectual property rights inside of the consortium.

Chapter 5:
Financial Services –
The Blockchain Innovation

N ot since the internet first came into existence have we seen such an awesome innovation as the blockchain. The technology behind the blockchain allows every person to hold transactions and to make them as strangers but in a way that is totally transparent. There is no intermediary between the person making and the person receiving the transaction and the whole process is so much cheaper and easier. We can apply the blockchain concept to the whole digital world that is involved in making any kind of transaction or exchange secure, and this doesn't just apply to the bitcoin. There is a wide range of companies and business models that are starting to appear, based entirely on the blockchain technology and these next couple of chapters will take you through a number of them.

As you already know, a blockchain network is made up of distributed servers, or nodes. Each node shares the information about the transaction. As much as it all may sound very confusing, in actual fact, it is so much easier to understand the impressive business models that are based on the technology.

So far you have seen that the distributed ledger is a record of transactions that cannot be erased. The entire computer network, across the globe, that runs blockchain software takes care of the maintenance and the performance of the whole blockchain network. On average, around 6 times every hour, a new batch of transactions that have been accepted is created and this I called a block. It is added to the chain and published across all of the nodes, allowing the blockchain software to decide when a specific transaction has taken place.

It is this very feature of the technology that has expanded in popularity amongst the developers, the large banks, and the entrepreneurs. Along with Santander, who are already investigating the use of distributed ledgers and blockchain technology in the bank, both JP Morgan and Citibank have also shown a great deal of interest in using the technology.

A lot of startup businesses are also building up their business around the technology and, as a result, venture capital firms like KPCB are beginning to become interested in investing in them. Startups like Coinmetric gather research and data on the quantitative and qualitative behavior of blockchains, while other companies, like BTCJam, provide loans that are bitcoin-based. Yet others that are built on the technology include BitPay, BlockCypher, and BitPagos. One of the more interesting of these startups is called, simply, Chain and it helps other businesses to build up financial products that are based on blockchain technology, using its own Bitcoin API. NASDAQ has picked this company to help run a pilot on NASDAQ Private Market using the blockchain technology.

Some Use Cases and Initiatives

It is very evident that financial institutions are keenly interested in blockchain technology. Santander, as we mentioned earlier, have already come up with 20 to 25 different uses and have also estimated that banks who use blockchain technology can cut their infrastructure costs by up to an impressive $20 billion every year. UBS and Goldman Sachs have also set up labs to research blockchain technology and its uses within their own banks.

Right now, although you may think that the financial industry is the main focus here, in actual fact, it is non-financial uses that are taking the limelight. Over 50 different startups have appeared in the non-financial use category and Blockchain Capital, who used to be known as Crypto Currency Partners, has already raised more than $7 million towards an investment fund, their second in fact, for ventures that are related to both bitcoin and blockchain technology that relate only to non-financial uses.

Right now, the startups currently in this sector are focused mainly on the Internet of Things, asset servicing, documentary trade and identity management and it will be interesting to see how governments adopt the use cases to streamline their processes and those of the public sector.

Chapter 6:
Blockchain Uses – Financial and Non-Financial

The use cases of the blockchain technology have been growing as each day passes. As such, there has been a large variety of ways to which we could link real-world assets toe the blockchain and trade them digitally. Proof of concept is already being run for some of the bigger trading commodities, like bars of gold, diamond, and silver, after they have been authenticated through the blockchain. Following those, we also have the provision of voting, the establishment of real estate ownership, etc.

Quite apart from the startup businesses, financial institutions like the banks have been investing in the decentralized system and many are actively experimenting and researching how the blockchain technology can be used. Below, we look at the broad applications that some companies are providing through blockchain technology, financial and non-financial:

- **Development of apps** – proof of module ownership within app development

- **Digital Content** – Proof of ownership for the delivery and storage of digital content

- **Ride-Sharing** – a value transfer based on points for ride-sharing

- **Digital Security Trading** – Ownership/transfer

- **Digitization of Contracts and Documents** – including proof of ownership in the case of transfers

- **Decentralized Storage** – using a computer network that is on the blockchain

- **Company Incorporations** – the digitization of incorporations and the transfer of ownership and equity

- **Decentralization of Internet and Computing Resources** – Including those that cover all homes and businesses

- **Home Automation** – a platform that links the home network and connected devices to the cloud

- **Digital Identity** – Provision of digital identities that are sued to protect consumer privacy

- **Escrow and Custodian Services** – specific to the gaming industry, e-commerce and load servicing

- **IT Portal** – Smart contract that executes the fulfillment of orders in manufacturing and e-commerce

- **Patient Records** – the decentralization of patient record management services

- **Digitization of Assets** – Helps to improve measures for anti-counterfeiting

- **Reputation Management** – to help users to engage and share reputation, collecting feedback as well

- **Prediction Platform** – a decentralized platform for share market prediction

- **Enabling Review Authenticity** – using endorsements that are trustworthy for employee peer reviews

- **Sale and Purchase of Digital Assets** – a marketplace for the sale and purchase of digital assets and proof of ownership

Chapter 7:
The Role of Blockchain Technology in Future Capital Markets

Blockchain technology has caused a real stir, particularly in the financial world. Many banks, venture capitalists, and other financial institutions are already looking into how blockchain technology can be used to store data and for other financial uses. One such financial industry is capital markets and it is here that the industry experts are showing the most enthusiasm and optimism about using blockchain technology to solve a number of issues.

Asset Movement

In order for assets to be moved from one financial institution to another, the ledger balances for the assets must also move. This is not an easy job and involves the use of several intermediaries. The more there are involved in the transaction, the more messages need to be exchanged and this results in even more updating of the ledgers required. In an average trade, there are already several intermediaries, including CCPs (central counterparties), exchanges, CSDs (central securities depositories, custodians, brokers and investment managers. In order for the accounting to be correct and for the transaction to be successfully completed, all of the intermediaries involved have to make sure their ledgers are updated based on the messages that are exchanged.

In essence, this means that whenever a transaction takes place, even more messaging needs to be carried out and this causes delays and adds to the total cost. On occasion, in order for a transaction to be completed and all the correct ledger updates made, the intermediaries may have to complete even more ledgers, such as securities borrowing, realignments or cash management. All this does is delay the transaction and is usually referred to, in capital market speak, as a settlement cycle.

So how can blockchain technology help? The creation of a shared flat ledger to process the transactions that happen between several intermediaries is the most important expectation of the capital market industry and will help in cutting both the time and the costs involved in each transaction. Using blockchain technology will also ensure that real-time asset transfers can easily be facilitated.

Financial industries can make use of blockchain technology to build shared flat ledgers that can easily be managed by processing nodes that are trusted. Through the use of digital signatures, the intermediaries will be able to update the ledgers to finish the business transaction. Shared ledgers have to be encrypted so that data confidentiality is maintained. The key processes that are involved in the execution of a trade, like trading, security clearance, settlement and clearing can easily be redesigned and made much simpler with the use of the blockchain.

Onboarding and Maintenance

Account maintenance and client onboarding is the next part of the capital market industry where blockchain technology is highly likely to be put to good use. KYC, or Know Your Customer, costs are incredibly high and cutting down on the cost and cutting out some of the KYC checks that need to be done is just what business the world over are looking to do. If they had a system built in the blockchain that both stored and facilitated Know Your Customer data, they can cut their costs and they can cut down on the amount of YC checks that need to be done. There are already a number of blockchain startup businesses that are focused on the improvement of identity management and we expect to see this number rise significantly over the coming years.

What About Payments?

Payments are a segment of the market where we can expect to see a substantial rise in the use of blockchain technology over the next few years. The blockchain technology can be used to customize the business rules for the processing of transactions, as well as help to tailor these rules to the specific business. This will all be based on the needs of the specific organization and the technology used would be open source software, enabling any number of businesses to use and tailor the software to their own requirements.

Areas that will see the biggest benefits of blockchain technology are bonds trading and OTC (over the counter) derivatives. The technology will be able to provide the business with a secure settlement model that is in real-time and is also cost effective to run, along with being decentralized and global. In short, it really is just a matter of time before the blockchain steps in and starts playing an immense role in capital markets.

A financial services company, based in Belgium and called Euroclear explains how blockchain technology can help the capital market sector. They say that, put basically, the records for every security would be placed onto a flat accounting basis, which means there would be "multiple levels of beneficial ownership" contained on each ledger. There would no more need to operating data normalization for reconciling internal systems or for agreements on exposure and obligation. There would be processes and services that are standardized, reference data would be shared, processing capabilities, like reconciliations, would be standardized, data would be near real-time and there would be a better understanding of the worthiness of counterparts. For regulators and other privileged participants, there would be better transparency on holdings data, along with a whole host of other improvements.

The Benefits for the Capital Market

According to Euroclear, the capital market segment would reap the following benefits:

Pre-Trade

- Better transparency of holdings

- Better verification of holding

- A reduction in credit exposures

- Mutualization of all static data

- Much easier KYC

Trade

- More secure transaction matching in real-time

- Immediate and irrevocable settlement of transactions

- Automatic cash ledger DVP

- Automatic reporting

- Better, more transparent supervision for the market authorities

- Higher standards in AML2

Post-Trade

- Real-time cash transactions do not need to go through central clearing

- Reduced margin requirements

- Reduced collateral requirements

- Interchangeable use of assets as collateral on the blockchain

- Automatic execution of all smart contracts

Securities Servicing and Custody

- Primary proceedings directly to the blockchain

- Automation of servicing processes

- De-duplication of servicing processes

- Better central datasets that have flat accounting orders

- Common data for reference

- Automatic processing of fund subscriptions and redemption directly on the blockchain

- More simplified method of fund servicing

- More simplified method of accounting

- Simpler methods of administration and allocation

Who are the Early Believers and the Pioneers of the Blockchain Technology?

On the Public Platform

1. **NASDAQ -** In December of 2015, NASDAQ released an official statement to say that Linq, its own blockchain ledger technology, had been successful in completing and recording a private securities transaction. This was the very first time this had been achieved using blockchain. NASDAQ Linq is a digital ledger that uses the blockchain to aid in the cataloging, issuance and recording of shares that are held in the Private Market by privately held companies. It is designed to complement the cloud-based capitalization management that NASDAQ Private Market, called ExactEquity. Linq clients will be given a full historical and comprehensive record of the issue and transfer of

their own securities, providing much better auditability,
governance of issue and transfer of ownership.

2. **ASX** – the ASX is the largest stock exchange in
Australia and it has now confirmed that it is working on
the development of a private blockchain in conjunction
with Digital Asset, a US-based firm, as a solution for
post-trade in the Equity market in Australia. The ASX
paid a sum of AUD $14.9 million to gain an equity
interest of 5% in Digital Assets Holdings and this fee
will be used to fund the first phase of the distributed
ledger solution.

On the Private Platform

1. **Chain.com** – Chain is a blockchain startup that
documents the use of the NASDAQ technology to issue
shares to a private investor. The issuer of the securities
used NASDAQ Linq to represent, in the digital sense, a
record of ownership. The settlement time was reduced
significantly and the paper stock certificates were, in
effect, redundant. Linq also allows investors and issuers
to complete subscription documents and then execute
them, all online.

2. **Funderbeam** – this company is set to launch the very
first investment trading platform that is based on the
blockchain technology in the next few months. They
will be doing this through a partnership with
ChromaWay, a developer of colored coins. Each of the
syndicates will be paired up with a micro fund and that
micro fund will own real stakes in real startups. As
such, when a member of the syndicate wants to trade

some or all of their own holdings, they will actually be trading digital stakes in the micro fund. The blockchain will be used to verify every transaction before it is enforced and the same thing happens when an investor decides to sell all or part of their digital stakes. In each of the investments, the change of ownership will have a distributed audit trail that is fully secure.

The Challenges Faced by the Capital Market in Adopting Blockchain Technology

The capital market will face a number of challenges that they will need to overcome if blockchain technology is to be adopted successfully:

1. **There must be very high standards set for the technology to succeed.** This is mainly for the security, for the performance and the robustness of the blockchains. Also, non-blockchain systems, like risk management platforms, will also have to be integrated at some point in the near future.

2. **Legislation and Regulations Must Be Upgraded.** In order for blockchain technologies to be successfully made an integral part of the infrastructure, new regulatory principles will need to be fully integrated.

3. **New Standards and Governance Will Be Required.** On some design points, industry alignment will be a requirement. Some of those points include whether the systems in use are fully open, like the bitcoin system, or whether they use a system of permission-based access; the principles that govern

whether the system is suitable for interaction with the ledger; whether different systems are interoperable – systems may be running difference safeguards against errors in coding or consensus protocols and this could create knock-on effects that may not be detectable to start with

4. **The Proper Management of the Transition to Minimize Operational Risk.** Operational risk is a big consideration and it must be minimized as far as possible.

Blockchain Companies Already Applying Distributed Ledger Security

These companies have already built their systems and are applying the blockchain-based distributed ledger technology to security and compliance

1. **Third-Key Solutions** – They provide cryptographic key management solutions and consulting to companies who use distributed blockchains, decentralized digital currencies and asset tokens

2. **Chainalysis** – provides products that let financial institutions spot the connections between two or more digital identities and develop lines of trust between them. The products can also help them to identify any malicious actors in the process. Chainalysis states that their mission is to come up with tools that stop any abuse of the system they are being applied to and that respect the privacy of users.

3. **Tradle** – uses the blockchain to bridge external and internal financial networks to achieve portability in KYC that is controlled by the user. An open-source mobile framework has been combined with business app development and a full integration platform that allows Tradle to develop sophisticated full-stack blockchain apps

4. **Vogogo** – This company specializes in providing verification tools for both payment processing and for risk management. To do this they use a simple JSON REST API.

5. **Elliptic** – the first company in the world to secure blockchain asset insurance and to achieve accreditation from one of the Big Four Audit firms, KPMG. They offer AML bitcoin protection in real-time

6. **Civic** – an identity solution that is based on the blockchain, aiming to tackle consumer identity theft and to bring about a reduction in online identity fraud.

7. **Coinalytics** – this company allows enterprises to determine real-time risk assessment and intelligence from the decentralized applications and from blockchains. They use methodologies that are based on pattern recognition and on real-time learning online to mine simulated data with few features.

8. **Sig3** – The company uses multi-sig technology to provide extra security layers for transactions made through bitcoin Instead of a requirement for just one signature or one key to make a transaction, the user is

able to set up a multi-sig wallet requiring the signature from two of three provided keys before the transaction can be completed and broadcast to the blockchain network. Because Sig3 is an independent automated third-party co-signer, it can be integrated into any multi-sig wallet while maintaining distance from said wallet. This ensures there is no point of failure.

9. **Blockseer** - This company has a mission to build a "unified foundation of transparency" for the public ecosystem for bitcoin. By providing the transparency of the blockchain and all of its participants, the company is aiming to cut down on the disorder and chaos and increase knowledge levels and analysis of the public blockchain network

10. **CryptoCorp** – This company is a security startup that is focused entirely on bringing about improvements to the bitcoin ecosystem. They offer a service that is called Digital Oracle, which can take part in multi-signature transactions that originate from any bitcoin wallet

11. **Blockverify** – A company that offers an anti-counterfeit system that is based on the blockchain. The system can be applied to luxury items, pharmaceuticals, diamonds and electronics and, using Blockverify, companies will be able to create their own product registers and monitor their own supply chains.

Chapter 8:
Blockchain Applications Beyond The FSI

lockchain fever is no way limited to the financial services industry, not by a long shot. As well as the banks and the financial tech startup companies, quite a few non-financial companies and industries have been paying quite a lot of attention to what is going on and are now looking for ways to make use of the opportunities that are offered by distributed ledger technology. In this chapter, we take a look at some of the most interesting examples of non-financial applications for blockchain technology.

Blockchain Technology and Commodities

The Real Asset Company allows people from all over the world to purchase silver and gold bullion in a secure and efficient way. They have an investor-friendly platform that is situated over the global vaulting infrastructure and which provides users with an online account for the purchase of silver and gold and for holding precious metal. Goldbloc is the gold-backed cryptocurrency used by the company that adds an extra layer of transparency and more control to the user's investment of gold. The company is backed up by a gram of gold and they fully believe that their cryptocurrency is the first step in bringing gold firmly back into the monetary system.

Uphold is another platform that is designed around the movement, conversion, transactions and holding of all forms of commodities or money. The business connects debit cards, credit cards, banks, and bitcoin to digital wallets for free transactions and financial services. Both consumers and businesses will be able to fund their accounts or by linking their credit or debit card or through bank transfer as well as bitcoin

Blockchain Technology and Diamonds

The diamond industry is probably the largest of all the natural resource industries and is a significant portion of the GDP in Africa and in other large diamond miners. The industry has one main hallmark – the fact that it is one of the most highly criminalized in the world. The stones are small and can easily be hidden and transported and the best bit about it for the criminal is that the transactions can take place in confidence and the sale will always return value over the years. Diamonds are well known to be firmly involved in the financing of terrorist activities and in money laundering on a massive scale the world over.

Because of the scale of the challenges with the diamond business, one of the technical pioneers, Everledger, is a company that provides an immovable ledger of the transaction verifications and identification for a number of stakeholders, from insurance companies right up to law enforcement agencies. Everledger assigns each diamond with its own digital passport that will accompany the stone through its transaction and also creates a unique fingerprint.

Blockchain Technology and Data Management

Factom is a leading and notable company in applying blockchain-based distributed ledgers to the non-financial sector, in particular, data management. Factom uses identity ledgers that are based on blockchain technology for data analytics and database management to support a number of different applications. Both governments and businesses can use Factom to make records management much simpler, along with easier record business processes. It can also be used to address issues surrounding security and compliance. Factom keeps a permanent record of all data in the blockchain, records that are timestamped, allowing companies to cut the complexity and the cost of auditing, records management and in complicity with government regulations.

Blockchain Technology and Cannabis

Serica is one of the blockchain companies that exists within the cannabis industry. They are responsible for bringing cryptofinance, software engineering, blockchain technology and financial custody to the traditional custodian finance model. The technology allows entrepreneurs to get their business set up legitimately, using the largest network of customers to grow their memberships, conversions, registrations and average order sizes. They use Secure Socket Layering (SSL) technology to encrypt all of the communication that takes place between Serica and the user's wallet. The blockchain is used to track every medical marijuana purchase and record them, giving the businesses the easy way to take online payments. Other companies that used blockchain technology in the cannabis business are Tokken and Hypur.

Blockchain Technology and Digital Content

Ascribe is a company set up to help creators and artists to attribute their digital art through the blockchain. Their marketplace lets digital editions be generated with unique IDs and digital certificates of authenticity as a way of proving authenticity and provenance. It also lets consignments from artists be accepted and digital works transferred to collectors with all the relevant terms and legal conditions. Other companies that do the same kind of thing include Stampery, Blockai and Bitproof.

Blockchain Technology and the Network Infrastructure

Ethereum is both a programming language and a platform that allows any developer to build next-generation distributed applications and publish them. The company can be used to decentralize, codify, trade and secure just about anything you can think of, including voting, financial exchanges, domain names, company governance, crowd funding, agreements and contracts, smart property and intellectual property, all thanks to the hardware integration.

Another company who offers up blockchain technology as a platform for the financial industry is ChromaWay. They are also working on building a smart contract platform that will allow workflows to be digitized and represented in a private, secure and efficient way.

Blockchain Technology and Market Forecasting

Augur.net is a decentralized and open-source platform for market predictions that is built on the Ethereum blockchain it lets users trade on event outcomes and then uses the crowd sourced information it gathers. Augur has plans to make use of decentralized public ledgers to create ways for anyone to tap into the forecasting power of the user base across the world.

Using Blockchain-based Platforms for Decentralized Applications

Previously we talked about use-cases under development for using the blockchain technology. In 2015, we saw what was undoubtedly one of the biggest spikes in investment and hundreds of different startup companies have appeared on the scene, all jumping on the blockchain bandwagon. One of the biggest phenomena was when multiple blockchain platforms were developed. These are platforms that will allow third-party projects to use to core infrastructure and come up with their own products and these have been spreading fast. While some are already light years ahead in terms of usage, others are fast catching up. Some of the most notable of these platforms on which projects or integrations are being built include:

- Ethereum

- Ripple

- Eris Industries

- MaidSafe

Blockchain

- Stellar

- Counterparty

Other platforms that are currently paving the way for these projects to be built include:

- Blockstamp

- Hyperledger

- Epiphyte

- PeerNova

- Koinify

- Chain.com

These are the blockchain-based platforms that have been vastly utilized by others who are looking to develop brand new projects or use-cases. While some of the financial platforms, such as Stellar and Ripple, have seen a major leap in partners in the area of developing gateways for transactions, Ethereum is the company that has dominated the non-financial use case, currently running around 14 separate projects on their platform

All of this just goes to show you how the blockchain revolution is already taking off and will very soon dominate the entire world.

Chapter 9:
5 Blockchain Technology Myths

It is very clear that the technology behind the blockchain is going to be the most important computing invention of this generation. This is because, for the very first time in the history of the human being, we have a full digital exchange for peer-to-peer value. Blockchain is a massive global platform and is firmly based on distributed ledger. It is responsible for establishing the rules, in the format of very heavy encryption and computations, that let at least two parties carry out transactions without the need for a centralized third party agency involved to establish the trust between the parties.

Instead of being reliant on government agencies, banks or any other intermediary to create that trust, the technology that fuels the blockchain ensures that trust is provided through clever doing and collaboration on a mass scale. The trust is actually built into the blockchain system and that is why the blockchain is otherwise known as "The Trust Protocol".

If we wanted to take that a step further, the blockchain plays several other roles. It is:

- An accounts ledger

- A database

- A sentry

- A clearing house

It is, in all likelihood, going to be the second-generation internet and it has the potential to take the economic grid and rewire it to run things for the better, shaking up the old and bringing in a completely new way of working. A fresh perspective on old business systems.

Sadly, there are still a lot of myths about blockchain technology doing the rounds and these are responsible for putting a lot of influential businesses and people off of using it. Here are the top 5 of those blockchain myths, busted and explained:

1. Blockchain is good but bitcoin is bad

There are an awful lot of people, particularly in the financial sector that are very excited about the potential that blockchain technology provides. However, those same people are under the misconception that digital currencies are not feasible, they are not desirable and are in fact quite dangerous.

The blockchain for bitcoin is a permission less system, which means that anyone is able to get into it through a device that has internet access and can interact with it in the same way they do the internet. Blockchains that are permissioned, on the other hand, require that all users have specific credentials, such as an operator's license for the blockchain they want to access, and those credentials are provided by a governing body or by the members of the blockchain. These permissioned systems use the distributed ledger technology but do not have any digital currency attached to them.

At first look, the permissioned or private blockchain looks like having several advantages. For a start, members of the chain are able to make changes to the rules if they want to. They are only required to get the group they are a part of to agree to make the change, rather than having to get an entire network involved. Costs are reduced because the transactions only have to be validated by the chain members, not by that massive network. All of this can also help reduce the costs of electricity, benefitting the environments and regulators are likely to prefer them over and over the public chain, like bitcoin, because there is no need to anonymity.

But, there are some things to consider. If it is easy to change rules, it is easy to flaunt those same rules. When you limit freedoms intentionally, neutrality can be severely inhibited. If the open value innovation goes, the blockchain technology will do nothing more than stagnate and vulnerabilities will open up in it. The bitcoin blockchain, on the other hand, and any other that is tied to digital currencies, include incentives built in to encourage users to validate the transactions.

2. **The financial services are the only real industry that will benefit from blockchains**

Provided they are able to locate the right leadership, the FSI can alter itself using the technology behind blockchain. That technology has the potential to completely revolutionize financial services, from the humble bank account and debit card right up to the entire credit card network. If everyone is sharing the same distributed ledger, transaction settlements can happen straight away for everyone. Banks could use blockchain technology to speed up the system process and reduce the massive costs they face every day. The smartest of them will strategically use the technology, and that includes the permission less system, to get into newer markets and bring a whole bunch of new services out.

But the FSI is only a small part of the whole system. Blockchains have the potential to disrupt those that are already seen as the disrupters, like Uber. Blockchains will be at the very center of the IoT (Internet of Things) and will allow the smart device to contract with, carry out transactions and share data securely peer-to-peer.

The blockchain has the potential to completely reinvent how democracy works by ensuring that politicians have to do something they are not used to doing – be accountable to the public.

3. Blockchains are B2B (business to business) and not for the general public

So many people are convinced that blockchain technology will turn around the economy and shake up our day to day life in more ways than we could imagine. They are not just for businesses, as others believe; the blockchain will have an effect on every man, woman and child in the world today.

4. There are too many issues with blockchains to make them work

There are those who say that blockchain technology really isn't ready for the world yet. It's too difficult to use properly and the best applications are still growing, still being developed. There are others who say that there is a huge amount of energy required to get consensus across the network. They ask what would happen when millions of blockchains all connected, are processing untold numbers of transactions every day. Are there sufficient incentives in place to get people to take part and not try to overthrow the entire network? Could blockchain possibly be the biggest killer of jobs for people of all time? Instead of seeing these are bad reasons for taking on the technology, we should perhaps be looking at them as challenges of implementing the system.

5. Satoshi Nakamoto is actually Craig Wright

Craig Wright is an Australian entrepreneur who has sensationally claimed that he is the original inventor of the bitcoin, Satoshi Nakamoto. We already know that Satoshi is the only creator; there were others involved. When the first bitcoin paper was written, and the first protocol, that was what got things started. Then that person disappeared off the scene, leaving the community to keep the work going. It is that community that is responsible for most of the blockchain code and all other bitcoin-related content. In that case, everyone in the community is actually Satoshi.

This is why it doesn't really matter who the original protocol. It is a permission less system and that means there will never be an arbitrator. For the next step to be taken, the entire community has to be the governor for things to move forward. The likelihood of Craig Wright being the real Satoshi Nakamoto is very slim though

Conclusion

Thank you again for purchasing this book! I hope this book was able to help you to understand what a blockchain is, the technology that underpins and the whole blockchain revolution and what it means for us.

The next step is to delve deeper into the world of blockchain technology and truly understand what the revolution is going to do for and to the world. Learn how it will revolutionize banking and financial industries, how it will have an effect on non-financial industries and how it will affect the security of future transactions.

You can see from the number of major companies and the number of startups that we have talked about in this book just how popular the technology already is. Companies like NASDAQ are not ones to jump into any old technology lightly, no without doing an awful lot of homework first and the very fact that they have gotten involved to the extent they have is a testament to the fact that blockchain technology is the future.

Bitcoin

—————— ❧❦❧ ——————

A Comprehensive Guide To Get Started With the Largest Cryptocurrency in the World

Mark Smith

Table of Contents

liable for any hardship or damages that may befall them after undertaking information described herein.

Additionally, the information in the following pages is intended only for informational purposes and should thus be thought of as universal. As befitting its nature, it is presented without assurance regarding its prolonged validity or interim quality. Trademarks that are mentioned are done without written consent and can in no way be considered an endorsement from the trademark holder.

71

Introduction

Congratulations on downloading *Bitcoin* and thank you for doing so.

The following chapters will discuss the cryptocurrency known as Bitcoin. Inside the pages of this book, you are going to learn how to use Bitcoin and how to invest in it. By the time that you are finished reading this book, you are going to have an innovative idea of how you can make money with Bitcoin.

Bitcoin is not an easy cryptocurrency to invest with but you are going to be able to do it.

Keep in mind that there is always going to be more that you can learn about cryptocurrency, therefore, you should never stop trying to find more for you to read and learn

There are plenty of books on this subject on the market, thanks again for choosing this one! Every effort was made to ensure it is full of as much useful information as possible; please enjoy!

Chapter 1:
Figuring Out What Cryptocurrencies Are

You may have heard of cryptocurrency, crypto currency, or crypto assets; the remarkable thing is that they are all the same thing. This is going to be a trade of currency that is going to utilize the controlling of units that are going to be created through negotiations. Cryptocurrencies are digital currencies that will cover topics such as Ethereum and Bitcoin. The very first digital currency that worked with a decentralized system was Bitcoin which happened back in 2009. Ever since Bitcoin came out, other cryptocurrencies have come out as well such as altcoins and Ethereum. Altcoins are going to be an alternative of Bitcoins.

Like it was just mentioned, the cryptocurrency program is going to be decentralized, and it is going to work on a blockchain where each negotiation will be located on a block. The fact that it runs on a blockchain makes it to where it is not going to run like a traditional bank. This is also going to make it different than typical banks because a traditional bank is going to run on a centralized system.

It was in 1998 that an anonymous electronic cash system was first published by Mr. Wei Dai which was called b-money. It

Bitcoin

was not too long after that, that bit gold came out by Nick Szabo which was released in an effort to work with solutions that are pieced together before they become published. The currency system is going to be based on the consumer's proof of work which made it to where the evidence of work could be reused. And, it was Hal Finney who collaborated with the currencies that Dai and Szabo came up with so that he could create Bitcoin, which is the cryptocurrency we know so much about today!

Bitcoin's founder was Nakamoto, and he used a cryptographic system that worked on the system of proof of work. Name coin was made to try and collaborate with a DNS and make it to where it worked off a decentralized system. However, by doing this, it made the internet's censorship harder. However, it did not take long after Namecoin was published that lite coin was issued. These types of cryptocurrencies ended up using scrypt so that they could operate properly. And yet again, a hybrid coin was born which was known by the name of Peercoin.

Although several platforms have been developed through the decentralized system does not mean that they were able to become successful and that is part of the reason that you do not hear of them nowadays.

In August of 2014, the United Kingdom stated that they were going to study how cryptocurrencies played an effect on the economy to see if it would be more beneficial to use cryptocurrencies. It was shown that using cryptocurrency was beneficial and you are going to be able to use cryptocurrency at some of the shops and restaurants that the United Kingdom has to offer. However, you cannot use it everywhere.

It was in the same year that the second generation of platforms for cryptocurrency was published. Some of these platforms were Ethereum, NXT, and Monero. These platforms offered some advanced operations that would allow the consumer to use smart contracts and stealth addresses.

Cryptocurrencies have also been known to threaten the price of credit for traditional financial institutions. There are more trades that are occurring with cryptocurrencies, and it is quickly becoming apparent that the customers of traditional banks are losing confidence in fiduciary currencies. This is going to cause a lot of difficulties to occur for the financial institution when it comes to gathering data to look and figure out what is taking place in the economy. This data is then given to the government in order for them to steer the economy in the direction that they want it to go.

One senior banking officer has said, "widespread use of cryptocurrency makes it more difficult for statistical agencies to gather the economic data that they require."

It was in February of 2014 that the first Bitcoin ATM was launched by Jordan Kelley who is actually the founder of Robocoin. The ATM is located in Austin, Texas and works just like a bank ATM, however, the scanners are going to read a form of government identification so that they can confirm the consumer's identity. The ATM is going to allow the user to gain access to the cryptocurrency that they have in their account once they have been able to verify their identity.

Chapter 2:
Bitcoin - The Oldest Cryptocurrency

With a blockchain, there are going to be public records that are going to be what is used when it comes to creating a new block. However, the best solution is not going to be to force a central authority into the system that will be trusted to make the proper decisions because the correct decisions are not always going to be made by that authority. When it comes to maintenance on the chain, it is going to be completed by the network through software that the blockchain is going to run on a regular basis. In other words, a live person is not going to have to run the blockchain, which is going to make it to where the human errors that occur can be decreased.

There are networks that will be used in validating the negotiations that are done so that they can be added to the ledger after the node has been marked by the system as available for broadcasting whenever the consultation is completed. With the proper verification, Bitcoin is going to take the data and distribute it to where it should be in the blockchain database. Therefore, every node that is used is going to create a new chain in the blockchain for every negotiation that a miner completes.

Bitcoin

A new block is going to be created six times each house or whenever the negotiation is accepted and verified on the chin. Bitcoin's software is going to aid in figuring out how much is owed to the miner so that the amount is not sent twice unless it is supposed to be. This is just another way to make sure that the blockchain does not overlook anything.

Blockchain ledgers are going to examine the data that has already been recorded for transfers that will be located in several distinct parts of the system so that they can be sorted out based on the notes that are tied to the negotiation or the bills that are located in a different location on the network. The cryptocurrency coins are going to be the only form of currency that cannot be spent on a block in the blockchain.

Anyone who is using blockchain to mine Bitcoins is going to have to create a new block so that it can be maintained until the mining has been completed and the reward has been sent out to the correct person. Miners are going to obtain awards for the negotiations that they complete once they have been verified and put on a block in the blockchain.

Chapter 3:
How to Store Bitcoins

B itcoin wallets are going to be similar to bank accounts because this will be where you store, receive, and send out Bitcoins. Keep in mind that just like your bank account, you are going to want to make sure that your wallet is secure so that no one is able to take away your coins!

There are several kinds of wallets that you are going to be able to pick from when it comes to Bitcoin. Software wallets, web wallets and various other ones. There are going to be pros and cons to each wallet, and you are going to be required to make sure that you are doing your research to discover the wallet that is going to be the best for you and what you are going to be doing with Bitcoins. It does not matter what wallet you choose; you will have to make sure that you keep your wallet secure as we just mentioned – and are going to continue to mention because this is extremely important!

Software wallet

1. Look at all of your options. Software wallets are one of the original Bitcoin wallets that were created. You will have all kinds of options to pick from when you are looking at using a software wallet. But make sure that you are picking one that is going to allow you to be in

complete control of the security of your Bitcoin because of how the software is set up. But, you are going to come across a huge hassle that is going to make it to where you have to install the software while making sure to maintain it properly.

    a. Being that blockchain is a public database, any negotiation that moves through the server is not going to be stored but will be verified as well.

2. The Bitcoin core wallet is the original Bitcoin wallet and has evolved as Bitcoin has evolved. There are a lot of people that are going to say good things about the Bitcoin core wallet while others are going to say dreadful things, but this is how it goes with everything that you are going to use. Going with the original wallet is sometimes going to be the best way for you to go. In order to download this wallet, you are going to need to go to www.Bitcoin.org and download the wallet application. Once the software has been installed on your computer, the portfolio's client is going to attempt to establish a network that way that it can begin to download the blockchain to the appliance.

    a. You will be required to have all of the blocks in the chain before you are going to be able to complete any negotiations with Bitcoin.

3. There are some other wallets that you can download if you do not want to use Bitcoin core. Every wallet is going to have good points and bad ones that are going to determine how the wallet functions not only on your computer but how it is going to interact with the

blockchain. For example, there are going to be some wallets that are going to only be available on Mac computers and it is going to have an app in the app store that will allow you to tie it to the wallet so that you can have access to your wallet and other Bitcoin services on your phone as well as your computer. The armory wallet is a wallet that is going to focus on security over other functions that other wallets may have.

    a. Each wallet will also have its own installation quirk.

    b. The hive wallet will be a wallet that is going to be geared towards beginners. Therefore, you may want to start with this wallet and move on to a different wallet once you have gotten the hang of using Bitcoin.

4. A lightweight wallet is not going to take up much space on your computer's hard drive as most other wallets will. These thin wallets are going to work faster since they will not be required to download the entire blockchain. If you want to use a lightweight wallet, you may want to consider using Electrum or MultiBit.

    a. You need to think about the fact that thin wallets are not going to be as secure as the wallets that are going to download the entire blockchain. So, if you do not want to lose losing your Bitcoins, you may want to stay away from a lightweight wallet unless you do not have enough room on your hard drive and this is the only way that you can get a portfolio for your Bitcoin.

Web wallet

1. You have to make sure that you understand how web wallets work before you decide that this is how you are going to want to store your Bitcoins. A web wallet is going to take a private key that is tied to your wallet and place it on a server that will be controlled by an admin group. There are going to be some web wallets that are going to allow you to link your mobile and software wallets together so that they are all in one place. This wallet is going to make it to where you can access it anywhere at any time as long as you have internet access, this is why web wallets are so popular. The website is going to be in charge of your public and private key which makes it to where Bitcoins can be taken without you knowing about it.

   a. There are a lot of web wallets that have security breaches; which is why you are going to need to research your wallet before you decide that you want to use it or else you are going to end up losing some of your coins without having the chance to get them back.

2. Whenever you pick out your web wallet, there are going to be a lot that say that they are focusing on keeping tight security for their consumers so that they can pull customers in. Some wallets you are going to want to bear in mind are Circle, Coinbase, and Xapo.

a. Coinbase will allow you to use it worldwide as well as giving you offers that you are only going to be able to use with Coinbase. They are also going to provide a trade service between the United States and Europe.

b. Xapo will be a simple wallet that is consumer friendly and going to offer some extra security that is known as a cold storage vault.

c. The circle will allow the citizens of the United States to link their bank accounts to their web wallets that way they can deposit money. When it comes to the consumers in other countries, they are only going to be able to use debit or credit cards.

3. You may want to consider using a wallet that is anonymous. The world of Bitcoin is going to make it to where you can stay completely anonymous which means that no one is going to know who you are. There are going to be some web wallets that are going to offer less security and are not going to offer you any insurance. A dark wallet is going to be an extension of chrome, and it is one of the most popular anonymous wallets. The servers are going to fluctuate to offer the stability that you need for your Bitcoins. But, the server is going to be vulnerable and is going to be open to being hacked at any time.

a. There are going to be a few anonymous wallets that are going to contain features that will offer faster cash outs than other wallets will.

Hardware wallet

1. You have to consider hardware wallets when you are looking at a portfolio to use for Bitcoin. If you are overly protective of your finances and your money, then you will want to go with a hardware wallet. A hardware wallet is going to be a physical device that is going to hold a private key and work electronically as well as be able to facilitate payments like any other wallet would be able to do. These wallets are going to be able to be carried on your person and will not require you to rely on a third party for storing your Bitcoins.

   a. A hardware wallet is going to be immune to any type of virus such as a Trojan virus that is going to steal your login credentials and credit card or online banking account details.

2. When you buy a hardware wallet, there are going to be a lot of different wallets that you are going to be able to choose from. They are going to range in quality as well as price range.

   a. A Pi wallet will use a cold storage method and is not going to have a wireless capability that you could be searching for. It is going to use the Armory client that the Armory wallet uses so that it is secure enough for you to work with without requiring you to set up your own wallet. It is going to be consumer friendly as well as be safe for you to use as a hardware wallet.

b. A USB wallet is going to be affordable and is getting to be more popular as a portfolio choice for those that use with Bitcoins. These devices will help to protect the data that you place on them and will contain a microprocessor chip that is going to be similar to the chip that a credit card is going to use. USB wallets are going to allow you to use it with different computers so that the device is connected through a secure connection.

c. Trezor is going to be similar to the Pi wallet, but it is going to have a small screen that you are going to use for interaction. There are going to be some private keys that you are going to be using because they are generated by the device. The Trezor is going to be immune to malware attacks.

3. Ensure that you are encrypting the wallet that you are using. There are a lot of hardware wallets that are going to require that you put a code or password in which will cause it to become encrypted whenever it is initialized. If your device does not require you to create a password for it, then you are going to want to think about it due to the fact that it is going to make your wallet more secure. Each hardware wallet will require a different protocol that you will have to follow so that you are establishing a secure encrypted connection.

Chapter 4:
To Mine or Not to Mine

When it comes to using Bitcoin, you will want to have coins in your account obviously because you are going to want to be able to spend those coins on goods and services. You are going to want to be able to receive coins for what you are doing as well.

You are going to be able to look up how you can mine Bitcoin online, but most of the guides that you are going to locate are going to be written for someone who has been using Bitcoin a bit longer than the average beginner. But, in this chapter, you are going to be able to learn the easiest way to begin mining Bitcoin so that you do not become too confused so that you can obtain some coins.

Find a Bitcoin mining rig

Before you can even think about mining Bitcoins, you are going to need to have an understanding that Bitcoin mining is going to be an extremely competitive niche to get into. There are going to be a lot of miners that are going to get into Bitcoin mining using some of the latest hardware that they are able to find which makes it more difficult for the average consumer to mine. Therefore, before you are able to start mining, you need to be able to figure out if mining Bitcoins is going to be worth it for you or not. This is not going to be anything that a program or another miner is going to be able to figure out for you. It is going to be a personal decision which is why you are going to want to make sure that you are doing the proper research.

There are some other tools that you can use to figure out if you are going to do good when it comes to mining Bitcoins by use of a Bitcoin calculator. You will need to enter the information from the miner that you want to buy and figure out if you are going to make a profit or if you are even going to be able to break even. There are a few miners that have discovered that you are going to need to put in a lot of money so that you can mine Bitcoins properly.

Once you have completed all of your calculations, you are going to need to purchase your miner. Make sure that you are not forgetting to go over all of the mining hardware reviews so that you are able to find the miner that is going to do the best job for you.

Remember not to get too caught up in the flashy programs that you are going to be able to download for mining because they are not always going to be the best. The best way to pick one that is going to work for you is to find the one that is going to have the best reviews by the miners that have used it.

Get a Bitcoin wallet

Just like we discussed previously, it is vital that you have a Bitcoin wallet. Since Bitcoin is a digital currency, you are going to need to have a place for it to be kept and you are not going to be able to send it to your bank account which is why you are going to need a wallet.

Once you have created a portfolio, you are going to get an address for that wallet. The address will be a long sequence of letters and numbers which is going to be considered the public address. You are also going to be given a private key. You are going to be able to give out your public address so that you can get Bitcoins from your mining as well as to other people if they are going to send you coins. However, do not give out your private key because the private key is going to allow someone to get into your Bitcoins and then you are not going to be able to get them back once they have been taken.

You may even want to consider using a self-hosted wallet which is going to contain an extra set that you will need to go through. Make sure that you are keeping a copy of the wallet's data file and print out the file so that it can be kept safe. This should be done on the off chance that your computer crashes and you cannot recover your records. In doing this, you are going to make sure that you are not losing your Bitcoins because once you lose them, they are gone forever.

Locate a mining pool

At the point in time that you have set your wallet up, you are going to have to find a mining pool to join. A mining pool will be a group of miners that are going to use the combination of their computing power so that they can try and make more Bitcoins. The biggest reason that you will not want to mine alone is that Bitcoin is going to reward in blocks at a rate of 12.5 at a time. Sadly, a lot of the time you are not going to be getting any of the coins that you mine.

Bitcoin

When you are working on a pool, you will be working with an algorithm that is smaller and going to be easier for you to solve due to the fact that everyone is going to be working on a portion of the algorithm and they will be working together to complete the larger algorithm. Bitcoin is going to spread out across the mining pool based on how much they contribute to solving the algorithm. Therefore, if you are consistent and do a significant portion of the work, then you are going to be able to receive a decent amount of coins.

But when you are picking a mining pool you are going to want to keep a few things in mind.

1. Is the pool stable?

2. What is the reward method?

3. What stats does the pool produce?

4. What is the fee for mining and withdrawal?

5. Is the withdrawal process easy?

6. How frequently is a block found?

When you are answering these questions, you will need to look at everything that makes a mining pool. Once you have signed up for a pool, you will get a username and a password for the pool that you will be able to use at a later date so that you can log into the pool and complete what you are assigned to complete for the algorithms on that block.

Get a mining program for your computer

Once you have completed everything that was mentioned above, you are going to be ready to start mining except for one thing. You will need to locate a mining client that is going to be able to run on your computer. You are going to be monitoring and controlling what happens with the mining rig that you have already gotten. Depending on the platform that you have gotten is going to end up depending on the program that you will need to get so that it is compatible with your rig. There are going to be some pools that will use their own software, and if you are going to join one of those pools, you are going to need to download that particular software. But, not every pool will have their own software, so it is an innovative idea for you to have your own software in the event that you join a pool that does not have its own software.

Begin mining

Now you can connect your miner to a power supply and start mining Bitcoins. You will have to make sure that you have hooked your miner up to your computer before you are able to open your mining software. However, after everything has been loaded, you are going to enter the name of the pool, the password, and your username so that you can get into the pool and start your mining.

You can start a collection shares that will represent the work that you do while you attempt to find the next block. Depending on the pool that you are using is going to depend on if you get paid for your share of work in coins, but you are only going to get paid if you have placed your address in the proper fields when you were signing up for the pool.

Chapter 5:
The Uncomplicated Way

Whenever you are investing with Bitcoin, you will have to obtain coins as we have already established that way you can use them at a later date to purchase things. There are at least five separate ways that you are going to be able to invest with Bitcoin.

1. *Mine coins:* This is a less common option whenever you are spending with Bitcoin. This is because it is going to involve that you solve complex mathematical equations and show your proof of work so that the chain can verify that you did the work properly.

2. *Trade coins:* There are going to be trades that you can locate online so that you can purchase coins. This is one of the more popular ways that people are going to get coins because you are going to be using traditional currency so that you can obtain digital currency. However, one of the issues with this type of negotiation is that it can take up to two weeks for a bank account to verify the trade and send the proper proof of identity. Whenever this happens, you are going to be waiting two weeks to get your coins, and at that point in time, you may forget that you have even purchased the coins.

3. *Buy face to face:* If you want to get coins quickly, then you are going to want to complete a face to face negotiation. But, this is going to very dangerous. There are stories that have made the news about people being robbed whenever they meet someone face to face so that they can get coins. Being that a single Bitcoin is going to cost at least a hundred dollars if not more, the bigger the investment, the more money that you are going to have to have on your person so that you can get a number of coins. Therefore, if you are going to have a face to face meeting, you are going to want to make sure that you are taking the same precautions that you would take if you were going to meet someone off of Facebook or Craigslist. Ensure that you are meeting in a public space and that you have someone with you so that you are protecting yourself and the other person.

4. *Face to face trade:* This is going to happen when a Bitcoin investor is looking for an easier way to get coins. A trade is going to be more complicated than a face to face negotiation. Face to face deals are typically going to be known as buttonwood meetups, and they will be similar to the trades that used to happen with the New York Stock.

5. *ATMs: A*n ATM is going to be the safest bet for you to get Bitcoins. It is important that you know that the Bitcoin machine will charge you a fee of five percent per negotiation and it is going to allow you to do a hundred thousand dollars' worth of negotiations if you have the money to complete them.

Chapter 6:
Keeping Your Bitcoins Safe

When it comes to Bitcoin, security is going to be extremely important and something that you are always going to want to think about when you are using Bitcoin.

The banking system is going to be like a garden that has been walled in. there is not going to be much that is going to happen to the money other than you are using it each day. Your bank is going to be responsible for making sure that the money is safe whenever you put it in their institution. So, if something goes wrong, your bank is going to have a number that you are going to be able to contact so that you can get the issue fixed or a chargeback initiated. You will not need to worry about any special procedures or backups when it comes to how your money is going to be handled. The only thing that you are going to have to worry about is spending your money on what it needs to be spent on.

But, this is going to be different when you are using Bitcoin. The biggest issue you are going to that a vast majority of consumers will not be used to the big shift that is going to occur when the responsibility for their money is shifted to them. This causes people to lose a lot of money even though they do not do it on purpose. It often happens because of simple mistakes that you are not going to know about until it happens. Plus, you are not going to be able to contact anyone once this error has been made so that your error can be fixed. When it comes to Bitcoin, you are going to be your own bank, and it will be on you to make sure you are taking care of the security of your Bitcoins.

Basic rules

It is not hard to go to your local newspaper and find a story about someone losing Bitcoin because of human error, technical error, or someone steals them. But, there are a lot of mistakes that you are going to be able to prevent by following some basic rules.

1. When you are using an online service such as the Bitcoin trade, you are going to need to be using a two-factor authentication. If you are not using a two-factor authentication, then anyone is going to be able to gain access to your account and steal your coins. The only thing that they are going to need is your account password. The scary thing is that this happens a lot. Attackers are going to get your password through a wide variety of techniques that hackers use. It could take the hacker a minute to get your password, but they are going to get it eventually. You need to check your account management settings for the account that you are using so that you can turn on the two-factor authentication.

Tip: when you are going through and setting up your authentication, you will receive a secret key that is going to be tied to a QR code that you are going to be able to scan with your phone through a QR scanner. You are going to need to print out your code so that it is on a piece of paper that you can keep in a safe place that only you have access to. This is going to make it to where you can make sure that you are the only one who can get into your account even if you lose your phone.

2. Ensure that you have direct control of your Bitcoins. If you do not have the private key, then you are not going to have control of your coins. Being that coins are stored in a wallet, that wallet is also going to have a private and public key just like we discussed earlier. A public key will be the address that you can give out to people so that they can send you coins. If you do not have your coins to the address that you have control of directly, then they are not going to be in your control. When that happens, you are going to end up losing the coins forever.

3. You should keep regular backups of your wallet. You should not have to be told to keep backups of your wallet, but there are going to be some people out there that do not think to back up their wallet. You should make backups with any critical data that you are working with, especially when that data is going to be dealing with money. It is an innovative idea that you have a safety net that is going to allow you to place your data on a hard drive just in case you lose your computer to a natural disaster or it crashes. Once your coins are gone, they are gone forever. No one else is going to get those coins; they are going to vanish into a space that no one is going to have access to.

Tip: you are going to need to look up a hierarchical deterministic wallet that is going to enable you to perform a single time backup. This backup is going to make it to where there are twelve to twenty-four simplehuman words that you are going to have to write down and place in a safe place so you can access it later. This will make it to where you are not going to be required to do regular backups.

Security challenges with Bitcoin

There are financial regulators that are figuring out that Bitcoin is going to have some significant financial losses when it comes the financial stability of the programs. Some of these liabilities include:

1. The distribution of the ledger system which is unregulated at this time by any financial regulators. Take for instance that there are some systems that are going to be more vulnerable to fraud caused by the collision of network participants.

2. An increase in trading delays. It has been clocked that most negotiations are going to take around forty-three minutes to complete.

3. There is the concern that Bitcoin could become a currency that is used by terrorists and cyber criminals which could end up to the government shutting Bitcoin down.

There are some negotiations that have not been able to be completed which causes them to remain unverified forever.

Chapter 7:
Proper Bitcoin Techniques

B itcoin is known as the very first digital currency that removed the middleman as well as found a way that they could go around the bank and its payment processors. Bitcoin is a market that is decentralized and is going to be spread out across the world making it to where virtually everyone can use it. The only thing that a consumer is going to have to have is a stable internet connection. Of course, there are going to be other things that a consumer is going to need in order for them to properly mine, but they were discussed in previous chapters and will be discussed again in this chapter.

1. *Get coins.* There are several ways that you are going to be able to get coins, and it is all up to you on how you want to obtain those coins. You can either buy coins if you have the money to do so. Or, if you are good at math, you can mine coins by solving mathematical equations.

2. *Get a Bitcoin wallet.* You do not have to know how a computer works inside and out or know any coding in order to know that you need to have an account where your coins can be stored safely. There is a lot of money on Bitcoin that a third party is not controlling and this

is one of the major benefits that you are going to find when it comes to using Bitcoin. Along with that, there will be some trades that are going to cost a million dollars, and all of the money will be what entices hackers to try and get into the system so that they can get the money for themselves. So, instead of putting your money in your mattress, you are going to be safer keeping your coins to yourself instead of trusting them to a Bitcoin trade. Any wallet that you find listed below is not going to require that a third party have any sort of access to your coins.

a. Mobile wallets

   i. Jaxx

   ii. Airbitz

   iii. BitPay

   iv. Mycelium

b. Web wallets

   i. Blockchain.info

c. Hardware wallet

   i. Ledger

   ii. Trezor

d. Advanced wallets

   i. MultiBit

   ii. Armory

3. *Obtain a public address.* Once the wallet that meets your needs, you will have to get a public address. You are going to need to wait for around twenty minutes to get a confirmation that tells you that you have completed the steps correctly. When you have gotten this email, you are going to see some coins placed in your wallet.

4. *Shop, give away, donate and invest every coin that you get in your possession.* The sky is going to be the limit when it comes to what you are going to be able to do with your coins.

    a. Give them to a friend so that you can show them how to use Bitcoin.

    b. Invest with Bitcoin. There are around twenty-one million coins that have been created in the blockchain, and the coins worth is going to increase. As an investor, you are going to have to hold your block and just wait for it to bring you money.

    c. You are going to be able to take your coins and convert them into gift cards for sites such as Dell or Overstock. There are going to be stores that are going to accept Bitcoin, but that will depend on where you live because not every store has caught onto digital currency yet.

    d. Donate your coins because just like spending your coins in stores, there are sites that are going to allow you to spend Bitcoins so that their site can continue to run.

And now you are going to be able to use Bitcoin. It may not seem simple when you are looking at it because there are going to be a lot of steps that you are going to go through but you are going to be able to do it.

You are going to have to get used to how the platform works and how things work before you are truly able to use Bitcoin. But, once you get used to it, it is going to be like anything else that you have to learn how to use. You will have a period of learning, and you are bound to make some mistakes, just make sure that you get over making mistakes before it is too late and you end up losing all of your Bitcoins.

One of the best things that you can do is make sure that you are learning from other people's mistakes so that you can try and save yourself some time.

Chapter 8:
The Bare Facts of Bitcoin

This section of the book is going to be where you are going to be where you get some of the basic facts about Bitcoin. There are some interesting facts that you are going to learn about Bitcoin in how it has grown not to mention it has some kind of interesting facts about how Bitcoins have been used ever since they were created.

1. *No one single entity controls the currency:* With traditional money, the bank is going to control it, and the worth is going to increase and decrease based on the market, not to mention you can physically hold it. But, Bitcoin is going to defy everything that traditional currency follows. Everyone who uses the Bitcoin technology is going to control it because they are going to be validating the activities of other miners around the world.

2. *There are a finite number of coins*: This is actually not true. Just because it does not have to be physically printed does not mean that there can be an unlimited number of coins because that would end up causing the worth of the currency to decrease and eventually causing it to become worthless. Instead, there are 21, 000, 000 coins on the Bitcoin blockchain.

3. *Bitcoins have no set worth*: Whenever you look at the traditional money, you are going to notice that it states how much it is worth. Except, money is going to have worth because we say it has worth. And, as Bitcoin becomes more and more popular, the more worth that is going to be placed on each Bitcoin.

4. *All negotiations can be seen*: One of the unique things about Bitcoin is that it is entirely transparent. The only thing that is not going to be transparent will be a miner's personal data. You are going to be able to see everything that is on the blockchain from the negotiations that are completed to the amount of those negotiations. This is supposed to install a level of trust and security amongst those in the Bitcoin community.

5. *Bitcoins: Y*ou will be able to mine Bitcoins by solving mathematical problems in order to verify negotiations from around the world. You will get coins in return for solving the problem.

6. *Reversals and payments:* You cannot be forced to pay on the Bitcoin platform, and you cannot take back a negotiation. Therefore, if you send a company Bitcoins, you are not going to be able to revoke the negotiation, and they cannot bill you again.

7. *Sending money: Y*ou are going to notice that if you send money to someone in a different country, there are going to be transfer and conversion fees that are going to be tied to it. Along with that, your friend is most likely going to have to wait a few days for the money to become available. But, when you are using Bitcoin, you

are not going to have to pay those fees and your friend is going to have access to the funds instantly.

8. *Lost wallet:* Whenever a wallet is lost all of the Bitcoins are going to be done automatically, and they are going to be gone forever. Since the blockchain is anonymous, you are not going to be able to claim that any of the coins are actually yours. So, whenever Bitcoins are lost, they are going to be removed from the circulation forever due to the fact that each Bitcoin is going to have a unique key that is tied to it.

9. *Digital wallet*: Just like when you log into your bank account to see your balance, you are going to have a digital wallet that you are going to be able to log into to see what your balance is.

10. *Bitcoin studies:* There are some universities that are now allowing their students to pay their tuition with Bitcoin even if they are not in the united states. Other countries such as the UK or Cyprus are following suit and offering another solution for their students.

11. *Bitcoin Boulevard*: In the Netherlands, there is a boulevard that is going to have a significant number of shopkeepers who will allow you to purchase goods or services with Bitcoins. There is also a Bitcoin Boulevard located in Cleveland, Ohio.

12. *Bitcoin's first negotiation*: There have been 43, 472, 379 negotiations completed on Bitcoin since it was created. But, you may be interested to know that the first consultation was set up by the technology creator

for Bitcoin, Satoshi Nakamoto, that completed the first negotiation by sending a hundred Bitcoins to Hal Finney in January of 2009.

Mr. Finney has been in the cryptocurrency community for a long time, and he has been working with PGP Corp for many years assisting them in creating one of the most famous encryption systems that you can find. Hal Finney launched one of the first anonymous remailers that was used to encrypt emails and it is now being implicated in Cypherpunks movement.

Hal Finney was quoted saying:

"When Satoshi announced the first release of the software, I grabbed it right away. I think I was the first person besides Satoshi to run Bitcoin [client]. I mined block 70-something, and I was the recipient of the first Bitcoin negotiation when Satoshi sent ten coins to me as a test. I carried on an email conversation with Satoshi over the next few days, mostly me reporting bugs and him fixing them.

After a few days, Bitcoin [client] was running pretty stable, so I left it running. Those were the days when difficulty was 1, and you could find blocks with a CPU, not even a GPU. I mined several blocks over the next days. But I turned it off because it made my computer run hot, and the fan noise bothered me. In retrospect, I wished I had kept it up longer, but on the other hand, I was extraordinarily lucky to be there, at the beginning. It's one of those glass half full half empty things."

13. *Million-dollar Bitcoin pizza:* May of 2010 a Bitcoin miner named Laszlo Hanyecz paid 10,000 BTC for two pizzas which are equal to around thirty dollars.

Chapter 9:
Making Bitcoin Easier to Use

As you probably have already figured out, Bitcoin is going to be a complicated platform for you to know. You are going to have to practice a lot and make sure that you are having a lot of patience so that you can find the proper mining pool and wallet that is going to give you everything that you are looking for. If you do not locate the wallet or pool that is going to meet all of your wants and needs, then you are better off waiting and doing more research till you can find the one that is absolutely perfect for you.

When it comes to buying or getting coins, you are going to want to make sure you are not going over your means, even if that means that you do a mixture of buying and mining.

In this chapter, you are going to learn some of the things that are going to be there to help make it to where you are able to use bitcoin a little easier. The whole point behind these tips and tricks is to make Bitcoin easier for you!

1. *Have two separate wallets.* You are not going to need to keep all of your coins in the same wallet if you are going to be spending them. Keeping them in a wallet that is known as your savings wallet and then having another wallet for all of your negotiations will make it

easier for you to try and keep hackers from getting your coins. The great thing about Bitcoin is that you are not going to have a limit on wallets that you are going to be able to have in your possession. It is not going to be hard for hackers to follow negotiation records to find out which wallets belong to the same people, but it is going to be harder to hack into the wallets and get all of your coins. You can even keep a few coins in multiple wallets so that you do not lose all of them.

2. *Savings and web wallets are going be hacked and and they will take all your coins away, leaving you empty.* Being that there is no way for you to truly show that the coins are yours which means that you are not going to get them back. A web wallet, while convenient is going to need to be used like a checking account. So, in other words, you are going to need to use a web wallet if you are going to be spending your coins sooner rather than later. The faster that you spend them, the less likely you are going to be opening yourself up to hackers to take your coins. You should remember that Bitcoin is not going to work like a credit card.

3. *Protect your privacy.* The private key that you get is going to be like your pin number for your wallet, and you are not going to give that out to people so why would you give out your private key?

4. *Cold storage makes it to where you do not need to keep your coins in a wallet or not.* No matter where the coins are, they are going to be open to attacks. Bitcoin wallet applications are going to save the data in locations that are predictable as well as vulnerable.

There are attacks that have been reported by the consumers of Bitcoin, and the most common solution solutions that you are going to find is that you are going to need to take your private key and keep it stored offline. Whenever you save your key offline, it will be saved as QR code, and you are going to have the ability to print it off onto a piece of paper or save it onto a USB stick.

Whenever you want to transfer bitcoins from a wallet that you have listed offline so that they can go somewhere else, then you are going to need to take that code and scan it before entering your key in the fields that require it. For some extra security, you are going to want to encrypt your private key that way they are useless if a hacker gets a hold of them. You will just need to make sure that you are not forgetting what your encryption password is or else you are out of luck.

Chapter 10:
Learn from Others

As it has been mentioned before, if you know some of the errors that other people have made, then you are going to be able to learn from them, and you are not going to have to deal with the heartbreak and frustrations of losing all of your coins.

Some of these mistakes may not be things that you would think to do. However, it is better to know about the mistakes so that you are saving yourself. It is going to be hard to learn from mistakes that others have made, but it is better to be aware of what has happened in the past than to just go blindly into the world of Bitcoins.

1. *Trade wallets:* Having a trade wallet is going to be one of the worst mistakes that you can make when it comes to trading coins. When you decide to use a third-party service to store your coins, you are going to be allowing yourself to become open to attacks from all directions. This happens because when the trade is hacked, or the trade does anything fraudulent, then you will not have the option of claiming your coins so that you can get them back. This is why you are going to want to obtain your own Bitcoin wallet for the coins that you get, or

else you are going to be opening yourself up to a lot of issues later on down the road.

2. *Price changes:* You have to remember that Bitcoins are still currency, even if they are a digital currency which means that it is going to be volatile. It is not going to be too uncommon for you to watch the price of Bitcoins to change a hundred dollars a day. This means that you should not panic if the price goes down. You will need to think of the long-term investments. The price is going to go up and down, but the platform itself is going to continue to go up. However, after you have completed a few trades, you are going to be used to the price fluctuations and it is not going to be a big deal when it comes to the cost decreasing.

3. *Currency changes*: There are various cryptocurrencies that you are going to have the option of investing with, and you are going to be able to trade back and forth between the currencies. But not every cryptocurrency is going to be as established as Bitcoin. Even Ethereum is not as established as Bitcoin is even though it is one of one of the bigger cryptocurrencies that have appeared ever since Bitcoin has come out. But, because there are other cryptocurrencies that are out there, you may find that you are tempted to float between each cryptocurrency. This is not ideal because when you are going to be losing your investments. So, you are going to want to remember that you should pick a coin and stick with it. That does not mean that you cannot have an account that mines Bitcoins and Ethereum. However, you are going to want to keep the trading between the two to a minimum.

4. *Education:* You can never know too much! You need always to be searching for what you can learn about Bitcoin because it is an ever-evolving platform. There are going to be new tips that are going to come out about the platform and how you are going to be able to use it so that it is easier for you in the long run. There are going to be some people out there that are going to place false information out there that is going to be meant to throw you off and make it to where you end up losing your coins. While this is not the wisest idea, it does happen. So, if there is any point in time that you find that you are confused if you are doing the correct thing or you are not sure if what you are reading is accurate, then you will be able to locate someone that knows about Bitcoin and get their opinion on it. Either that or you can go onto a Bitcoin form and find the answer for yourself.

Chapter 11:
Scams Are Everywhere

Being that bitcoin is so popular, it is going to be easy and common for people to try and create scams that are going to be aimed at consumers so that they can try and get money out of Bitcoin users. However, there are some scams that you are going to want to keep your eyes open for so that you do not become a victim. The more that you know about the scams you may come up against, the better that you are going to be able to protect yourself from them.

1. *Ponzi ploys and high-yield investments:* These scams are going to be meant to bring people in by promising them of high-interest rates on the deposits that you make. Anyone who invests initial is going to be paid out by the investors that come along at a later time. Whenever the new investors stop joining, the payments can no longer be made which means that the ploy ends up collapsing. These scams are typically going to last a few months if they are lucky, but, the people that are behind the ploy are going to come back and repeat the process again even if it is at a later date.

2. *Mining investment scams*: A mining scam is going to involve the verification of negotiations so that it is ensured that there is going to be security for those using

the public ledger. These processes are going to typically involve orders for equipment where you are going to pay for the equipment beforehand but you are not going to receive anything. When these types of scams are carried out, a powerful and expensive computer is going to be required to keep track of all of the "orders."

3. *Wallet scams*: As it has been mentioned in previous chapters, a wallet is usually going to require some sort of software program that is going to allow you to store coins. Wallet scams are going to be where consumers are told that they can make a transaction that has more anonymity. You will have to place enough coins into your wallet and the scammer is going to take those coins and move them to their own wallet, and you are never going to see them again.

4. *Trade scams:* A trade scam is going to pull a Bitcoin consumer in by offering a credit card processing rate that is going to be more competitive than other competitors. The trade is not going to give anything to the Bitcoin consumer once payment has been sent.

5. *Phishing scams:* Phishing scams are going to be scams that come through your email informing you that you have won Bitcoins. Once you click on the link that is in the email, you are going to put your wallet information in and instead of you getting the coins as you think that you are going to get, you are going to be giving your coins to the person that sent out the scam.

Avoiding scams

It is highly advised that you ensure that you are investigating every company that you are looking into for Bitcoins. You are going to want to make sure that they are completely transparent in what they have to offer. Should there be any place in their business plans or services that you cannot see everything that is involved in the process the company is most likely going to be fraudulent and, you are going to want to try and stay away from them.

There are going to be some public audits that you are going to be able to find that will assist you in avoiding any doubt when it comes to ensuring that a company is delivering on everything that they have to offer. A proof of reserve audit is going to be made so that you can force a company to disclose their Bitcoin holdings publicly.

Make sure that you keep in mind the old saying "if it looks too good to be true, then it probably is." When you are dealing with Bitcoins, you need to make sure to treat it as you would cash. Protect it and do not just leave it alone for others to steal.

Chapter 12:
Setting the Facts Straight

S ince people do not completely understand Bitcoin, they are going to cause a lot of myths to pop up so that they can try to understand it. However, with all of these myths floating around it is not only hard for you to know what the truth is but also can scare you away from using Bitcoin.

But, in this chapter, you are going to learn about some of the more common myths that you are going to hear about Bitcoin. You should know the truth about Bitcoin or else you are not going to be able to use Bitcoin effectively. Once you understand the truth, the blockchain platform is going to be easier to understand and use!

1. *There is nothing new about Bitcoin; it is going to be similar to other currencies found online.*

    With this being said, that means that Bitcoin is going to

    a. Be able to be printed at the whims of the consumer.

    b. The arbitrary rules are going to be able to be imposed upon by consumers through controllers.

   c. If the central point of control is attacked, it can be destroyed.

But, since Bitcoin is decentralized, it is going to solve all of these problems.

2. *Bitcoin is not going to solve problems that fiduciary currency and gold currency are not able to solve.*

While gold is great, Bitcoin is going to be

   a. Easy to granulate

   b. Can easily be moved.

   c. Is easy to verify

   d. Can easily be secured.

Fiduciary currencies will hold some significant dissimilarity to Bitcoin as well by making Bitcoins

   a. Non-Debt based

   b. Predictable yet limited in supply

   c. Unable to be controlled by a central authority

And, because there is an electronic fiduciary system Bitcoins are going to prove to be better than it by

   a. Being cheaper when moved.

   b. Remaining anonymous for consumers

   c. Lessening the transfer time

    d. And will not freeze

3. *Various entities are going to be able to change the features of Bitcoin to suit themselves.*

As long as the Bitcoin economy uses node wallets, then the features are not going to be able to be changed. The negotiations are going to be irreversible and will not be censored as long as no group of miners has more than fifty percent of the hash power and that all negotiations have the proper number of confirmations.

Bitcoin is going to require some features to be enforced so that it can continue to be a good form of money. Such as:

    a. You cannot violate any of the rules that are put in place to make sure the system is working properly.

    b. Money cannot be created out of nothing.

    c. The same coin cannot be spent twice.

    d. Coins cannot be paid without the consumer's private key.

The rules just stated are going to be what defines Bitcoin. The node software that is used will verify that the rules of Bitcoin are being enforced as they should be. If a negotiation happens to break the law will not be an intense negotiation on the blockchain, and it is going to end up being rejected.

4. *There is a processing power the backs Bitcoin.*

To think that there is no processing power behind Bitcoin is a lie. The currency is backed whenever it is tied to something else with a central party with an individual trade rate, but you are not going to be able to exchange Bitcoins for computing power that was used in the creation of those coins. Think of Bitcoins like gold; it is not backed by anything either. The Bitcoin currency will be created through processing power, and its integrity is going to be protected by a network that already exists.

5. *Bitcoins are worthless since they are not backed by anything.*

Some people are going to argue that gold is not backed by anything. But, there are features built into Bitcoin that are going to result in the system allowing the coins to be subjectively worth by other people. The Bitcoin valuation will be demonstrated by an individual that is free to trade for or with Bitcoins.

6. *The Bitcoin worth is going to be based on electricity and computing power that is used in the mining process.*

You are going to see that this statement is going to be applied to the labor theory of worth. This theory is going to be accepted as false most of the time. Just because a set of Bitcoins takes so many resources in order to be created does not mean that the Bitcoins are going to be worth that amount. They can be worth more or less depending on the utility of the consumers.

More to the point, the causality is going to end up being reversed from what the theory says. How much it costs to mine Bitcoins is going to depend on how much the coin is worth. Should they go up in value, more people are going to mine them which is going to cause the difficulty to go up, therefore, the cost of mining is going to go up as well. The opposite is going to happen whenever the prices of coins go down. This is going to balance out any effect that mining is going to cause in order to always charge an amount that is going to be proportional to the worth of the coin.

7. *Bitcoin has no intrinsic worth.*

Sorry, but this is not true. Every Bitcoin is going to give the holder the ability to be able to embed large numbers in short negotiation messages which are going to occur on a global distribution level and will also be time stamped permanent data store such as the blockchain. There will not be data stores that are similar to the one where your negotiation will be retained. But, there is going to be a tradeoff between the number of messages that are created and how quickly they are going to become embedded. Back in December of 2013, it was fair to state that a single Bitcoin was going to allow for around a thousand messages to be embedded all within ten minutes of the message being sent. Therefore, a fee of 0.001 BTC was enough to get the negotiation to be confirmed. The message that was embedded would have intrinsic worth is that it is going to be used in proving ownership of the document inside of the negotiation. Whenever you look at the electronic notarization services, you are going to be charged ten dollars a record which is going to produce an intrinsic worth of 10,000 dollars per Bitcoin.

There are going to be other tangible commodities that will have intrinsic worth, and the worth is typically going to be less than the trade price. Think about gold. If you do not use it as an inflation-proof store of value, but only use it for industrial purposes, then it is not going to be worth as much today being that industrial requirements for that piece of gold will be smaller than the supply that is currently available.

It does not matter what event is happening, historically the intrinsic worth and other attributes are going to be used in helping to establish commodities as mediums for trade, but it is not going to be a required prerequisite. In this sense of speaking, Bitcoins will lack intrinsic worth, but they are going to make up for it by possessing other qualities that are going to be required in making it a good medium for trade.

8. *Bitcoin is not a legal tender. Therefore, it is illicit.*

It was in March of 2013 that the United States Financial Crimes Enforcement Network set out some new guidelines that focused on decentralized virtual currency, specifically Bitcoin. Under these new guidelines, "a consumer of virtual currency is not a Money Services Businesses under FinCEN's regulations and therefore is not subject to MSB registration, reporting, and recordkeeping regulations." So, when a miner is mining coins for personal use, they are not going to have to register as an MSB.

Generally speaking, there are going to be a lot of currencies that exist and are not going to be backed by the government. When you look at it, currency is nothing more than a unit of account. There are going to be national laws that are going to change country to country, and you are going to want to check what your jurisdiction says on trading commodities such as digital currency.

9. *Bitcoin is going to cause domestic terrorism due to the fact it is only going to harm the economic stability of the USA and its traditional currency.*

When you look at how the united states define terrorism, you are going to notice that it says that you have to commit violent acts for illicit purposes in order to be considered a terrorist. Since Bitcoin is not domestic to any country because it is a worldwide community, it is not going to be illicit. Also, you are not going to use it for illegal activities, so you are going to be safe. If anything, bitcoins are going to help promote the economy since there are going to be those that are going to use actual currency in order to purchase coins.

10. *Bitcoin is going to allow tax evaders to continue to evade the law.*

When a cash negotiation is completed, it is going to hold the same level of anonymity but will be taxed. You are the one who is going to be responsible for ensuring that you follow your state and country laws when it comes to Bitcoin or else you are going to have to face the consequences that come with breaking those rules.

Chapter 13:
Questions That Are Frequently Asked About Bitcoin

1. Can Bitcoin be used for illicit activities?

Well, seeing as Bitcoin is money and money have been used for legal and unlawful activities all throughout history, then technically yes it can be. However, Bitcoin surpasses any bank or credit card in their crime against unauthorized uses of money. Bitcoin has created innovative payment systems, and these systems have more benefits than they do drawbacks.

Bitcoin was designed to make money more secure and to act as a protection against financial crime. Take for instance that Bitcoins are not able to be counterfeited. A consumer is going to be in complete control of their payments, and there are not going to be charges that just randomly show up like what can happen with a credit card.

Some big concerns are that Bitcoin is going to attract more criminals being that it is used in making payments that are not only private but irreversible. However, what most people do not realize is that these features are found with cash and wire transfers. Bitcoin is subjected to regulations that are similar to those that are already in place for financial systems that already exist.

2. *Does Bitcoin have the option of being regulated?*

The protocol that Bitcoin follows is not going to be able to be modified without all of the consumers agreeing on all of the decisions. Should special rights be assigned to a local authority to govern the rules of the Bitcoin network then it is going to result in a catastrophe because it is not possible in a practical sense.

Organizations that are rich can invest in hardware used in mining in order to control half of the computing power of the network which will give them the power to block or reverse negotiations that are recently made. But, there is no guarantee that this power is going to be kept by them because it is going to require an investment that is larger than all of the other miners that are on the Bitcoin blockchain.

It is possible to regulate Bitcoin's use though. Bitcoin has the option of being utilized for a great number of things, and some of this stuff are going to be considered illicit based on where the miner is located and the laws of that jurisdiction. Bitcoin should not be thought of in any other way other than a tool that can be subjected to the regulations of the area in which it is being used.

The restrictive laws can make it difficult to use Bitcoin which is going to cause it to be hard to determine the percentage of consumers who are going to continue to use the platform. Also, the government can decide that they want to ban Bitcoin in order to prevent domestic businesses and markets from shifting into other countries. The biggest challenge is going to be to develop solutions that are going to be efficient and effective without impairing the growth of the new markets and businesses that are starting up thanks to Bitcoin.

3. Is Bitcoin subjected to taxes?

Since Bitcoin is not a fiduciary currency, it is possible that you are not going to have to pay taxes on Bitcoin. But, keep in mind that there is a lot of legislation in place that can cause a tax to be put on Bitcoin.

4. What is Bitcoin's consumer protection?

Bitcoin is allowing people to break free of traditional banking and learn how to complete negotiations on their own. Every consumer is going to have the option of sending and receiving payments in ways that are going to be similar to cash, but they are going to be through contracts that are a tad more complicated than simply working with money. There are going to be several signatures that are required in order for a negotiation to be accepted and it will only happen if a particular number of people allows the negotiation to be signed. This is going to allow for dispute mediation to be developed and take place for future negotiations.

These services are also going to enable third parties to approve or deny negotiations in the event that there is a disagreement between the parties, but the third party is not going to have control of the money that is placed in the middle of the dispute. Unlike cash and many other payment methods, Bitcoin is going to leave public proof that the negotiation did indeed take place which is going to open up the door to businesses getting caught for fraudulent practices.

You should also take note that merchants are typically going to depend on their public reputation in order to stay in business and pay their employees, but they are not going to have access to the same information when it comes to dealing with new customers. Bitcoin is going to allow for individuals and businesses to protect against fraudulent chargebacks while offering the customer the option of asking for more protection when they are dealing with a merchant that they may not particularly trust.

5. *What is going to determine the price of Bitcoins?*

The price is going to be decided by the supply and demand of Bitcoins. Whenever the market goes up, the price is going to increase, and whenever it falls, the price will fall. There are going to be a limited number of Bitcoins that are in production, and the new coins are going to be created at a rate that is not only decreasing but predictable as well. This means that the demand is going to continue to follow the level of inflation in order to attempt to keep the price stable. Since Bitcoin is still a small market, it is not going to take a lot of money to move the market in one direction or another which is why the price of Bitcoins is still volatile.

6. *Can Bitcoins become worthless?*

Yes. There are all kinds of stories about the various currencies that have failed over time, and now they are no longer used. Just because other currencies have failed mainly due to hyperinflation which is not possible with Bitcoin. But, there are technical failures that can occur. A good rule of thumb is that no currency is going to be absolutely safe from any failures. While Bitcoin has proven to be stable since it started, there is still a lot of room for Bitcoin to grow or to fail. No one knows what the future of Bitcoin is going to bring.

7. Is Bitcoin a bubble?

Just because the price goes up fast does not mean that there is a bubble. When an artificial overvaluation occurs, it is going to cause a sudden downward correction which is going to constitute as a bubble. There are going to be choices made based on a human's action and as more and more miners make decisions, the more the price is going to fluctuate and cause the market to try and seek some sort of price discovery. There are going to be reasons for these changes which can end up causing miners to lose their confidence in Bitcoin.

One of the biggest dissimilarity s between price and worth will not be based on the fundamentals of the economy, but instead an increase in press coverage, which will, in turn, stimulate demand, a sense of uncertainty, and greed.

8. Is Bitcoin a Ponzi ploy?

Since a Ponzi ploy is going to be an operation that is going to be based on fraudulent investments. The payments are only going to be returned to the creators of the scam. Ponzi ploys are meant to attempt to collapse whenever the last investor is gone, or there are not enough new investors.

Bitcoin is not going to have a central authority which means that no one is going to be in the position to make fraudulent representations about how investments are returned. Just like any other major currency, you are not going to have the promise of getting purchasing power as the trade rate moves around freely. This is going to cause the volatility for the owners of Bitcoins and will cause them to either make money or lose money at an unpredictable rate.

9. What about the initial adopters of Bitcoin?

Those who are considered initial adopters have a significant number of coins because they took liabilities and invested their time and resources in the technology that was not yet proven and had hardly anyone using it. Not only that, but it was harder to secure the program at that time. So many of the first customers took their coins and spent large amounts a few times over before they became valuable, or they bought small amounts and did not make any large gains. There are not going to be any promises that the price is going to increase or decrease. This is going to be similar to when you invest an initial startup that will either gain worth or never break through. While Bitcoin is still considered to be in its infancy, you are going to notice that it was built to last long term. This makes it to where it was difficult to imagine how less biased the program can be towards initial adopters and while today's consumers which may or may not become the initial adopters of tomorrow.

Conclusion

Thank you for making it through to the end of *Bitcoin*, let's hope it was informative and able to provide you with all of the tools you need to achieve your goals whatever it may be.

The next step is to start your blockchain account and start investing with Bitcoin.

Hopefully, you are able to get a decent return with mining or investing in Bitcoin so that it is not a waste of your money and time. Just remember, investing, and mining are going to be hard when it comes to Bitcoin. Therefore, you should not be discouraged if you do not become rich because the chances are that you are not going to get rich with Bitcoin. However, it can be a new financial investment for you.

Finally, if you found this book useful in any way, a review on Amazon is always appreciated!

Thank you and good luck!

Finally, if you found this book useful in any way, a review on Amazon is always appreciated!

Ethereum

----- ❧❦❧ -----

A Comprehensive Guide For Ethereum And How To Make Money With It

Mark Smith

Copyright 2017 by Mark Smith
- All rights reserved.

liable for any hardship or damages that may befall them after undertaking information described herein.

Additionally, the information in the following pages is intended only for informational purposes and should thus be thought of as universal. As befitting its nature, it is presented without assurance regarding its prolonged validity or interim quality. Trademarks that are mentioned are done without written consent and can in no way be considered an endorsement from the trademark holder.

Table of Contents

Introduction

These days, it may seem like every time you open your computer, there is an ad or some kind of feed regarding Ethereum or its virtual currency, the Ether. Many people have heard of Ethereum and its counterpart, the Ether, but few people understand what Ethereum actually is. This ebook is designed to answer your questions about what Ethereum is and how it works.

Ethereum was created by a Russian-Canadian teenager named Vitalik Buterin. It is basically a blockchain on which developers can create a particular kind of app known as a decentralized application, or Dapp. Its underlying genius is the use of something called the smart contract, a contract written in code that is enforced without the use of a third-party mediator. The Ether is the currency used to power the Ethereum network.

This ebook will guide you through all of the basics of Ethereum. It will begin by explaining in more detail what Ethereum is and what smart contracts are. It will then explain what blockchain technology is and how blockchain is used in the Ethereum network. After that, it will show you what Gas and Ether are and how they work. Next, it will go through some applications that run on Ethereum to help give you a feel for what kind of apps Ethereum is best-suited for. Finally, it

Ethereum

will give you some ideas for how you can make money on Ethereum.

If you are ready to understand what Ethereum is and how you can make money on it, then this ebook is definitely for you!

Chapter 1:
What is Ethereum?

Vitalik Buterin and the Founding of Ethereum

Vitalik Buterin was born in Kolomna, a city near Moscow in Russia, in the year 1994. His father was a computer programmer, and his mother was a business analyst. When he was six years old, his family moved to Canada in search of employment opportunities and a better life. As a young child, Buterin quickly discovered his interest in mathematics and its applications in computer programming; in fact, he was a mathematical genius. He was able to quickly add large sums in his head, something that not only most young children but even adults have difficulty doing.

When Bitcoin was first released in 2009, Buterin was only 15 years old. Two years later, when Bitcoin was beginning to gain some traction, his father introduced him to it. He became the co-founder of *Bitcoin Magazine*, and was also one of its primary contributing writers; he remained there until the middle of 2014. He also wrote about Bitcoin in other publications, including the scholarly, peer-reviewed publication *Ledger*, which provides information on blockchain and cryptocurrencies.

Ethereum

In 2013, when Buterin was 19 years old, he went to a conference on cryptocurrency in San Jose. While some considered cryptocurrency to be another pending dotcom boom and bust, Buterin decided that the movement was real and he wanted to be a part of it. He was in school at the University of Waterloo, but he dropped out to pursue Bitcoin interests.

When Buterin returned home to Toronto, he wrote a white paper on a new blockchain idea that he called Ethereum. In June 2014, he was awarded a $100,000 Peter Thiel Fellowship, which he used to develop Ethereum.

The idea immediately took off and was an instant success. Ethereum quickly became seen as an alternative to Bitcoin, and Buterin was featured in Fortune's 40 Under 40 list.

The Ethereum Network

Ethereum is an open-source network that is built using blockchain technology (for more information on what blockchain is and how it works, see the next chapter). It enables individuals, businesses, and other entities to develop their own decentralized applications.

Dapps. A decentralized application, also known as a Dapp, is a new concept that works differently than traditional applications, such as Gmail or most online banking websites. These traditional applications are centralized, meaning that they are connected to one main server. If that one main server fails, the entire network will fail. Furthermore, the server acts as a type of "middleman" that all transactions must go through in order to be processed. Because a Dapp is decentralized,

144

there is no main server to process transactions. Rather, it is open-source, meaning that anyone is able to access the code. Further, no one person is able to hold a majority share of the application, so any changes made to it must be by a popular consensus of the Dapp's users.

According to the white paper that Vitalik Buterin published for Ethereum, a Dapp must meet five conditions. It must A) be open-source and autonomous so that no one person or entity controls the majority of it, B) have any protocol changes agreed upon by all users, C) store all of its information in a public blockchain, D) use a cryptocurrency native to the blockchain on which the Dapp operates (meaning that a Dapp that is built onto the Bitcoin blockchain must operate using Bitcoins, and a Dapp that is built onto the Ethereum blockchain must operate using Ether), and E) must generate cryptocurrency tokens using a predetermined algorithm.

One example of a Dapp is Alice.SI, which holds charities accountable for actually making an impact by doing the charitable work that they claim to do. The Dapp works through smart contracts (see the section below on smart contracts) to ensure that donations to charities are only processed if the charity actually does the work it promises. Another Dapp is Coakt, which has taken crowdfunding beyond raising money to also raising talent and technology to support people's ideas and goals. In order to fully access many Dapps and use them to their full potential, users must use an Ethereum-compatible browser, such as Mist.

Dapps have their own advantages over traditional applications, and some have even said that they are the next step in the evolution of computer technology. One advantage is that because there is no centralized server that Dapps connect to, there is no central point of failure; if one server that the Dapp connects to fails, there are plenty of other servers that will keep it running. Another advantage is that the applications are cryptographically secure inside a blockchain network. Therefore, they are inherently protected against things such as hacking and other fraudulent activities.

There are three main types of Dapps, with each type containing its own subtypes. The first type of Dapp has its own blockchain. Examples include networks such as Bitcoin, Ethereum, Litecoin, Lysk, and other networks that run on their own cryptocurrencies. The second type of Dapp is built onto a blockchain and runs similarly to a software program. It runs on its own rules and protocols and uses the tokens of the blockchain onto which it is embedded. The third type of Dapp is built onto the second type of Dapp to develop a more specialized type of software. Each type of Dapp serves a different purpose and provides a different type of contribution to the people that it serves.

In his white paper, Buterin proposed three types of Dapps that would be powered by the Ethereum network. The first type would power financial applications and provide the users with trustless ways of managing their money and processing transactions. Examples include things such as savings wallets, cryptocurrency exchanges, wills, and even some employment contracts. The second type would be for semi-financial applications; a semi-financial application is one in which money is exchanged but most of what is involved is not monetary. The third type is what Buterin called "Governance Applications," and refers to applications that do not involve any kind of financial transaction. These applications can be used for functions such as voting in governmental elections and providing decentralized governance.

In many ways, Dapps are still in their infancy. The concept is still being explored by programmers, and some innovators are looking for new ways to exploit the technology to further revolutionize how computing can be made safer and more secure in this digital and information age. Applications such as online voting are still a long way away, and the general public is not fully aware of what Dapps are and how they can be beneficial over traditional apps. As Ethereum gains more traction in the coming years, the full potential of Dapps will undoubtedly be more fully explored.

DAO's. Buterin also envisioned that Ethereum would enable and support the creation and use of DAO's. A DAO is a Decentralized Autonomous Organization that can be used to handle financial transactions without any middleman or breach of trust. Rather than being a brick-and-mortar company, it is entirely embedded in computer code.

DAO's are notoriously hard to define because they can exist in a multitude of forms. As a general principle, though, they function as digital ledgers that are timestamped embedded in a blockchain. Therefore, they are next to impossible to alter and must be carried out. For more information on how this works, see the section on Smart Contracts and the chapter on Blockchain.

The DAO was a company designed to leverage the use of DAO's and was built into the Ethereum blockchain in 2016. However, a weakness in the code used to create it was exploited, and $55 million dollars was siphoned off the network. In response, Ethereum created a hard fork in its network to help restore the viability of the blockchain and replace the funds that had been lost.

Smart Contracts. Smart contracts are a concept that was initially envisioned by Nick Szabo in 1996. Nick Szabo arguably came up with the concept of cryptocurrency over a decade before Satoshi Nakamoto created Bitcoin in 2008-2009, and some believe that he may actually be the legendary figure. Smart contracts are, in some ways, an extension or natural evolution of the blockchain technology that was used to create Bitcoin and later Ethereum. In fact, they are largely used in facilitating the exchange of cryptocurrencies.

A smart contract is a computer protocol that is intended to create and enforce the execution of financial and other transactions. It is extremely similar to a DAO in many ways. When two parties agree to enter into a smart contract, the terms of the contract become embedded as a block in the blockchain. The block is timestamped, and because more blocks are subsequently added to the blockchain, going back to retroactively change the smart contract is impossible (for more information on how blockchain works, see the chapter on Blockchain). Furthermore, that block becomes publicly visible; instead of a middleman, such as an escrow service, ensuring that the terms of the contract are carried out, the entire network of users on the blockchain serve as witnesses to the contract's veracity. However, the identities of the people involved in the contract remain anonymous. When both parties have completed their duties and the terms of the contract are fulfilled, the smart contract releases whatever has been held.

For example, imagine that Bob and Joe want to exchange Bitcoin. Bob has one Bitcoin that he wants to sell for $4000, and Joe agrees to buy it. They draw up a smart contract, and according to its terms, they have one day (exactly 24 hours, at which time the smart contract will expire) to complete the transaction. Bob transfers the Bitcoin into the smart contract, and Joe transfers in the $4000. At the end of the 24 hours, the smart contract releases the $4000 to Bob and the one Bitcoin to Joe.

In many ways, smart contracts are the driving vehicle behind the Ethereum network. Their trusty nature and complete anonymity has drawn many people to Ethereum, and many of the Dapps on the Ethereum network function largely by using smart contracts.

Ethereum vs Bitcoin

Ethereum has been described by some as a rival to Bitcoin. After all, its digital token, the Ether, soared in value — by over 4000% — just in the first half of 2017! Bitcoin has long dominated the cryptocurrency scene, and has also grown substantially in the year 2017. However, some anticipate that the value of the Ether may surpass that of Bitcoin over the next few years.

There are some key differences between Ethereum and Bitcoin. Satoshi Nakamoto's concept of Bitcoin was the impetus behind his invention of blockchain technology, and Vitalik Buterin worked extensively with the Bitcoin community before creating Ethereum. The biggest difference is that Ethereum was not primarily designed for the creation, distribution, and facilitation of the Ether cryptocurrency.

Rather, it was designed to enable entities to develop Dapps onto the blockchain. The Ether was created to help enable the execution of the Dapps (for more information on how the Ether works, see the chapter on Gas and Ether). Bitcoin, however, was not created to power a network. It was created exclusively as a cryptocurrency. In other words, Ethereum is a network for computer programs, while Bitcoin is exclusively a cryptocurrency. Therefore, the Ether is connected to an actual "product," while Bitcoin exists entirely autonomously.

The next few chapters will better explain some of the mechanics behind how Ethereum works, including what blockchain technology is, how Ethereum uses it, and how the Ether works.

Chapter 2:
Blockchain

Blockchain is the technology behind the creation of cryptocurrencies, most notably Bitcoin, and was used by Buterin to create Ethereum. Buterin realized that while blockchain was created for Bitcoin, its uses went far beyond cryptocurrency.

The concept was initially laid out in Satoshi Nakamoto's white paper on Bitcoin, which was published on October 31, 2008. The technology was actually developed as a means of facilitating the cryptocurrency that Nakamoto envisioned. To better explain how blockchain works, this chapter will take a historical look at how the ideas that lead to the development of the technology evolved into the powerful networks used today.

History of Blockchain

During the 1980s, computer technology advanced to the point where many entities were using software that allowed altering and modification of photographs; the growing, extensive use of this software raised questions about how to protect data and sensitive information from tampering and how to ensure that it had not been altered. Two computer programmers, Stuart Haber and Scott Stornetta, proposed a solution that they published in an article entitled "How to Time-Stamp a Digital

Document," which was published in the *Journal of Cryptology*. Their solution was that rather than timestamping documents, business should timestamp the actual data that is transacted. The method that they proposed would ensure that the data contained in a digital document could not be modified. Their method was the foundation of blockchain's digital-ledger feature, which prohibits the altering of data in transactions.

A few years later and into the 2000s, a Cambridge University expert in cybersecurity named Ross Anderson advocated the need for a paradigm shift in how computer security works. Current computer security models were extremely vulnerable to security breaches and hacks; infamously, many hacks were directed at government and military servers, and some hacks directed at commercial companies siphoned off millions dollars and exposed personal information of many customers and clients. The need for an entirely new model of cybersecurity was an important impetus behind the creation of blockchain, which did not build on other models of computer security but rather created an entirely new paradigm.

More innovative ideas continued to come from leaders in computer programming. At the time, they did not revolutionize programming, but they continued to lay the foundation for the eventual creation of blockchain. For example, in 1998 a programmer named Michael Doyle filed for a patent that would create new security protocols using chain-of-evidence protocols, along with public and private keys to ensure that the data being transacted was not subject to tampering. His system ensured that data was accurately timestamped without any need for third-party verification. The system that he developed helped create blockchain's trustless feature, which refers to the fact that no trust in a third party or middle man is required for someone to make a transaction on the blockchain.

The same year that Michael Doyle filed for his patent, Nick Szabo, an expert in digital contractual law, developed a model for a digital currency that he referred to as "bit gold." Users would solve complex mathematical problems to "mine" the cryptocurrency, and the solutions to those problems would be used to create the next set of problems. Bit gold was never actually developed, but the methods that Szabo proposed developed the concept of a peer-to-peer network. A peer-to-peer network is one in which users must collaborate with each other rather than rely on a centralized entity to confirm transactions. The peer-to-peer network is an essential feature of blockchain, as it is the primary way of enforcing the trustworthiness of the network.

Three men named Charles Bry, Vladimir Oksman, and Neal Kin filed for a patent in August of 2008 for a new encryption technology that they had developed. This technology would require the use of public and private keys — as conceived of by Michael Doyle ten years earlier — to encrypt the information that was being transacted. The patent was for an almost exact model of blockchain, but all three men deny any connection to the mysterious Satoshi Nakamoto.

On October 31, 2008, an individual writing under the pseudonym of Satoshi Nakamoto published a white paper about his conception of using cryptocurrency. He named his cryptocurrency Bitcoin, an amalgam of "bit," referring to the unit used in computer science, and "coin." The name alluded to the fact that it was to be a currency that would exist entirely in a digital form rather than being printed as cash or minted as coins. In January of 2009, Nakamoto released Bitcoin and with it, the blockchain technology that sustained the network.

As previously mentioned, blockchain was developed originally for the creation of Bitcoin. However, its uses go far beyond Bitcoin, as Vitalik Buterin realized when he decided to create Ethereum.

How Blockchain Works

Blockchain is an entirely different method of computer programming. It did not improve on previous models but rather created a new paradigm for both programming and security.

Traditional computing models have an application that connects directly to a central server. For example, if you want to make an online purchase from a retailer whose online platform uses the traditional model, your transaction will have to pass through a central server. If the central server has failed for whatever reason — maybe there is too much web traffic or it is being worked on — your transaction will not be completed, and you will have to try again later. If your bank uses the traditional model for its online services and you want to access your financial information online, if the central server has failed, you will be unable to accomplish your goal. Not being able to access your bank information when you need it, especially in this increasingly digitized world, can have catastrophic consequences for your personal finances. Furthermore, the traditional model is extremely susceptible to hacking. A hacker merely needs to get into the central server, and then all of the information contained in that application is at his or her disposal. This information can include vast amounts of money, credit card and bank account information, social security numbers, and numerous other pieces of compromising and vulnerable personal information. As you may be able to see, the traditional model is outdated and not secure, as Ross Anderson took great pains to point out.

The blockchain model does not rely on a centralized server but rather an entire network of hundreds, if not thousands, of users who power the network. These users are able to verify the transactions that have occurred; in fact, a critical number of users are required to verify transactions before they are completed. This decentralized model has several implications. One is that the network is not controlled by any one person or entity but rather by the people who use the network. Another is that the network is virtually impenetrable to hackers, as in order to gain access to the network, every single user would have to be in conclusion to bring it down.

Below are some of the features of blockchain; understanding these features will help you understand the mechanics of how blockchain works.

Public ledger. At its core, blockchain is essentially a public ledger. A ledger is a collection of transactions that have occurred, usually kept by an accountant. Ledgers may be kept in software programs such as Quick Books and only be visible to authorized persons, such as the accountant, CEO, and any auditing service. Other interested parties, such as shareholders and employees, may not have access to the ledger and therefore be unaware of the company's financial health. Secrecy about the company ledger was a critical factor in the

2000 collapse of Enron, which caused many people to lose all of their money.

As a public ledger, anyone on the blockchain is able to view the transactions that have occurred or that are in process, albeit with anonymity regarding the parties involved in the transactions. Therefore, no one person is able to alter the data in any way.

Each transaction that occurs is recorded in a block. When a new transaction occurs, it is recorded in a block that is connected to the previous one. The connected blocks together form a chain, hence the "blockchain." This is why blockchain is essentially a ledger, and because it is visible to the public, it is a public ledger. In order to change the data contained in one of the blocks, one would not only need the collusion of every single user on the network but would also have to retroactively change every single block that comes after the block to be changed.

In Ethereum, each smart contract occurs as a block in the blockchain. Therefore, the terms of the contract must be carried out by the parties involved, and no one is able to retroactively change the contract.

Nodes. A node is a client computer on a blockchain network that processes and verifies transactions. Rather than one centralized server, blockchains usually have hundreds, if not thousands of nodes, which are usually operated on a volunteer basis. Some blockchains, such as Bitcoin, are seeing the number of nodes on their networks decline; to help solve this problem, Bitcoin is making plans to put nodes in outer space!

Peer-to-peer network. Because a blockchain network is decentralized, instead of a central authority regulating it the users themselves are the authority. They must work together and agree upon the transactions that have occurred, whether those transactions involve exchanges of cryptocurrency, mining (to be explained later in this section), or the execution of a smart contract. If the users on the network do not agree on a transaction, it is considered to be invalid.

As previously explained, the peer-to-peer network inherently provides such a high degree of cybersecurity that it is virtually impervious to any hacks or data tampering.

Timestamps. A timestamp is a record of the exact time at which a transaction occurred. They are essential in business and legal environments because they ensure that certain data existed at a particular time. One ubiquitous use of timestamps is the practice of clocking in for work. Businesses usually have an established protocol to ensure that employees are at work at a certain time so that they can be compensated accordingly. Tampering with timestamps can cause serious legal ramifications.

Blockchain technology relies on the use of timestamps to ensure the authenticity of transactions and utilizes Satoshi Nakamoto's method for ensuring that the timestamps are tamper-proof. As soon as a transaction occurs and a block with the transaction's data is created, that block is timestamped before becoming permanently embedded within the blockchain. The timestamp cannot be changed unless the entire network decides to make the change and every single block in the blockchain that has been created after that transaction is also changed. While there is presently no legal precedent, the consensus seems to be that a blockchain timestamp will hold up in a court of law.

Public and private keys. Public key cryptography is an essential blockchain feature because it helps prevent any fraudulent transactions from occurring. Users on a blockchain network have both a public key and a private key; the public key is visible to anyone, but the private key must be kept absolutely secret. When one user wants to make a transaction with another user, he or she will use that person's public key to send the transaction. The sender's private key will be used to encrypt the transaction so that it cannot be received by anyone except the intended recipient. The recipient will use his or her private key to open the message.

If a user's private key was to be exposed, someone would be able to access that person's account and make transactions. In the case of virtual currency, such as Bitcoin and Ether, the private key could be used to siphon off the person's entire holdings.

Hashes. Hashes are an important part of the blockchain's verification protocol. A hash takes a mathematical input of any size, runs it through an algorithm, and returns an output of a fixed size. The probability of any two hashes being the same is extremely low. Hashing is one way of keeping hackers from being able to access accounts on the blockchain. The following sections on proof-of-work and mining and forging will help you put the concept of hashing into the context of how it works in a blockchain.

Proof-of-work. A proof-of-work system is basically a method of proving that work was done to produce a transaction, meaning that the transaction was not made by bots. In a proof-of-work, a group of transactions are grouped together into a block, which is verified by a group of miners (see the below section on mining). The hash value from the preceding block is applied into an algorithm of the new block that is waiting to be verified, thereby creating a complex mathematical problem for miners to solve. The first miner to solve the problem is usually rewarded with a certain amount of cryptocurrency. In the Bitcoin blockchain, the difficulty of each block's problem is adjusted so that only one block can be solved (or mined) every 10 minutes. When the problem has been solved, the transactions inside the block are considered to be verified.

Ethereum has found that the proof-of-work system is extremely costly, both in terms of time and energy, so it has designed a new protocol called proof-of-stake. Proof-of-stake has the same goal and outcome as proof-of-work (ensuring that all transactions are legitimate), but it functions through a different process. There is no reward for the miners; rather, they take the transaction fees that are included in each Ether transaction. In a proof-of-stake protocol, the hash from the previous block is still applied into an algorithm. However, instead of miners competing to solve the complex mathematical problem that is generated, the creator of the new block (i.e., the miner who solved the problem) is chosen randomly based on the amount of wealth (i.e., stake) that that person has.

Mining and Forging. Mining is the process whereby new coins of the cryptocurrency used by the blockchain are created. It was developed by Satoshi Nakamoto as part of his proof-of-work protocol. Miners compete with each other to solve the complex mathematical problems that are created during the proof-of-work process. When the problem is solved, the block is considered to be mined. A set number of Bitcoins are released into circulation, with the miner receiving a portion of them as a reward.

Because Ethereum uses proof-of-stake instead of proof-of-work, it uses a process that is referred to as forging (referring to the process that blacksmiths use to create a new metal-based piece). Forging is similar to mining, except that new Ether tokens are not created when a block is solved. Rather, there is a fixed amount of Ether in circulation. While miners take a commission of the virtual currency that is created, forgers only take the transaction fees.

Ethereum virtual machine. Every time an Ethereum transaction is performed, thousands of node computers in the Ethereum network must collaborate in order to process the transaction. The transaction is written into a smart contract, which is then translated into a bytecode. The bytecode is read by the computers in the network using the Ethereum virtual machine, or EVM. Essentially, the EVM is a program used to interpret the bytecode. The EVM and miners running the nodes reject smart contracts that have not been paid for and ensure that no one is able to spend the same Ether twice.

Benefits of blockchain. Perhaps the most obvious benefit of blockchain is its security. Because of the peer-to-peer nature of a blockchain network, it cannot be hacked. All of the data on the blockchain is visible to everyone in the network because it actually relies on the people in the network, rather than a centralized authority (such as PayPal or MasterCard) to verify the transactions. This feature means that the network is transparent; there is no question about whether financial information is being recorded accurately and ethically. Another benefit of blockchain is that the data cannot be manipulated in any way; again, this is because there is no centralized authority. Any attempt at tampering with the data or manipulating the protocols would have to require the consensus of the blockchain's entire community!

Challenges of blockchain. While the benefits of blockchain cannot be understated, there are some challenges associated with it that will need to be met in the coming years to ensure its viability. One such challenge is how blockchain transactions should be viewed in a court of law. Because the technology is relatively new, as of right now there are few legal precedents regarding how the data in blockchain should be viewed legally. Another challenge is the energy required to run a blockchain network. Because hundreds, if not thousands, of computers are required to run the network, the carbon footprint created by blockchains is enormous. Estimates are that by the year 2020, Bitcoin will use as much energy as all of Denmark! One transaction on the Ethereum network uses as much energy as a typical family uses in a day and a half. This energy challenge can be met by providing incentives to users who use green energy to power their computers.

Another challenge associated with blockchain is the time required to complete a transaction. Because of the intense verification process, one Bitcoin transaction can take anywhere from 10 minutes to one hour. This can be a problem for users who want to use Bitcoin to buy a cup of coffee! Ethereum has met this challenge by establishing a new yet equally intense verification process, which has cut down the transaction time to about 12 seconds.

Chapter 3:
Blockchain and Ethereum

Like the Bitcoin concept that inspired the creation of Ethereum, all transactions made on the Ethereum network are part of the blockchain. The users are all linked together in the peer-to-peer network and collaborate with each other to make transactions.

How to Make an Ethereum Transaction

Before you can create a smart contract on Ethereum, the first thing that you need to do is create an account. Ethereum runs by using the Ether cryptocurrency (for more information, see the chapter on Gas and Ether), and all transactions require the use of Ether. This is to ensure that developers create strong codes and the people running the network are properly compensated. In order to use the Ethereum network, you may need the Mist Internet browser.

To create an account, you need to create a wallet that will allow you to store, send, and receive Ether. The wallet is like your gateway into the Ethereum network; in addition to managing your Ether, it allows you to write and execute smart contracts. First, you will need to download the wallet; this process will actually connect you to the entire Ethereum blockchain. Go to www.ethereum.org and scroll down the page until you see a link to download the Ethereum Mist Wallet. Clicking on this link will immediately begin to download the wallet as a zip file. You will need to unzip the file and then launch it.

After the launch is complete, you will be asked whether you want to use the test network or the main network. The test network is a sandbox; a sandbox is a program that runs only some of the computer's resources. This way, if a code on the program proves to be defective, only the resources used by the sandbox will be affected. The rest of the system will be unharmed. If you choose to use the test network, no Ether will be required. Use of the main network, however, will require Ether; the program will assist you in acquiring some.

Next, you will need to create a password. This password is used in creating your private key for sending and receiving transactions, so protecting it is of vital importance. Choose a strong password that other people will not be able to guess. Make absolutely certain that you remember your password, as it cannot ever be changed.

You will then be directed to your account's main page. At the top of the screen, you will see links labeled Send, Contracts, and Balance. You will also see in the middle how many nodes in the blockchain you are synced to. Below, you will see a bar that says Main Account. Below that is a string of numbers and letters; that is your public key, which is used by other people when sending you Ether.

To send Ether to someone, click the Send link at the top of the screen. Type in the public key of the person to whom you wish to send Ether and the amount that you wish to send. Next, you will be taken to a sliding scale to determine the maximum amount that the transaction will cost; this amount is paid to the miners who process the transaction. If you want to send the transaction as cheaply as possible, you will pay less but wait longer because with less money, the miners have less incentive to process your transaction. If you wish to send the transaction as quickly as possible, you will pay more but the transaction will be completed in just a few seconds. You will then enter your password to confirm this transaction; even though you must use your password to access your account, this feature adds in an extra layer of security.

How an Ethereum Transaction Works

A transaction on the Ethereum network can seem relatively straightforward to a user who is trying to exchange Ether or create a smart contract. However, the actual mechanics behind the transaction are actually quite complex. Here is an overview of what happens behind the scenes.

When making a transaction, the sender uses the public key of the intended recipient. Remember that the public key is visible to anyone; however, the private key (which is generated from the password) must be kept absolutely secret.

When the transaction is sent, the data becomes embedded in a block, which is connected to the block that came before it. It is now part of the blockchain, and is visible to everyone on the network, albeit without the identities of the users involved. The data in this transaction is included with data from other transactions in the block. The hash value from the preceding block is applied into a complex mathematical problem, which the miners (or forgers) must solve in order for the transactions to be verified. The solution is used to generate a hash value, which becomes applied to the next block in the blockchain. The miners are rewarded with the transaction fees that were paid by the senders.

The intended recipient will receive a notification that he or she has received Ether. He or she will log in to the account and receive the money.

Chapter 4:
Gas and Ether

The crucial difference between Bitcoin and Ethereum is that Bitcoin is a virtual currency and nothing more. It has an exceptionally high value that continues to increase and has shaken up concepts of what money is and how it should be regulated. However, it is not connected to an actual commodity. Think of it like gold: The price of gold is not connected to any particular good or service, and it is not as subject to things like inflation as standard currency, such as the dollar, is. Its value is based on how much people are willing to pay for it; in other words, the price of gold is determined by its demand. The demand for Bitcoin is high, so its value is also high.

Ethereum is not a virtual currency; rather, it is a commodity. It is a network that allows users to create and execute smart contracts, as well as develop their own Dapps. Running this network is rather costly; think of how much energy is required, considering that it is maintained by a system of thousands of node computers. Furthermore, there is a need to ensure that the Dapps created on the network are made efficiently and to the highest standards. Therefore, money is involved, ensuring that people are properly compensated for their work. That money comes in the form of Ether.

What is Gas?

Gas on Ethereum is similar to the gas that is required to run your car. The amount of gas that you need to put in your car is directly proportional to the amount of energy required for you to drive your car to your desired destination. If your car is a gas guzzler and you are making a cross-country trip (something that environmentalists would strongly advise against), a lot of energy will be consumed. Therefore, you will need a lot of gas. If you drive a Prius and are taking a weekend getaway to a beach that is two hours from your house, very little energy will be consumed, especially compared to the gas guzzler going across the country. Therefore, you will need much less gas.

Transactions on Ethereum take a lot of energy. They don't only require the energy required to power the computers on the network, but also the human energy required in the mining (or forging) process. After all, the miners need an incentive to process a transaction.

One thing that is important to note is that nobody owns Ethereum, not even the creator, Vitalik Buterin. The fees paid for gas do not go to fund a wealthy CEO's fourth vacation home. Rather, they pay for the workers on the network to do their jobs.

Some transactions on Ethereum, such as sending Ether, are relatively simple and straightforward. Other transactions, such as creating a new Dapp, are much more complex. Think of the simpler transactions as Prius cars and the more complex transactions as SUVs from the 1990s. A simple transaction requires less energy and therefore less gas. A more complex transaction requires significant amounts of energy and therefore a lot of gas.

One feature of gas in Ethereum is that the user gets to determine how much to pay for gas. While the amount of gas required to perform a transaction is the same (just as the amount of gas required to drive your car to a particular destination won't change), the amount of money that the user *pays* for the gas is up to him or her. Think of this scenario as different gas prices across the country; in some parts of the country, like California, gas is a lot more expensive than in places like the American South. Imagine being able to live in California while only paying as much for gas as someone in Mississippi! However, there is a catch.

When you send a transaction, you are given a sliding scale of how much you want to pay for gas. On one end is the cheapest option, which will usually take longer to process because, with less money involved, the miners have less incentive to process it. On the other end is the fastest option, which is more expensive but gives your transaction a priority spot inside its block. It is processed much faster because the miners have a higher incentive. If the transaction does not have enough gas, then like a car that runs out in the middle of the highway, the transaction stops before being processed.

How Does Gas Work?

Chapter 2 briefly explained the Ethereum Virtual Machine, or EVM. The EVM is basically a mechanism for running codes on the Ethereum network. It functions as a sandbox, meaning that it only uses a minimal amount of a computer's resources. Sandboxes are ideal environments for running test codes, because if there is a defect in the code (such as a virus), only the limited resources used by the sandbox will be affected. The EVM is used by developers to execute their test codes before they become integrated into the main Ethereum network.

In addition to testing codes, the EVM is an essential part of Ethereum's verification process. All transactions pass through the EVM, which is connected to every node on the Ethereum network. Think of the EVM as Ethereum's World Computer. Every operation on the World Computer uses gas; the amount of gas used is connected to the complexity of the operation involved. The fees from the gas go to pay the miners, to compensate them for their work in keeping the network going.

What is Ether?

When fueling up your car, you probably pay for the gas in dollars (or British pounds sterling, or Euros, or whatever fiat currency you use). When fueling up on Ethereum, you pay for the gas in Ether. Ether is the virtual currency tied to the Ethereum network. However, its soaring value has caused it to gain traction outside of Ethereum programmers, and even the mainstream media is picking up on this phenomenon. While Bitcoin is still the leader in the world of virtual currency, the Ether is growing at a faster rate. In fact, some analysts anticipate that within the next few years, the value of the Ether will surpass the value of Bitcoin!

Before explaining what makes the Ether unique, it may be helpful to fully understand what cryptocurrencies are. First, you need to understand what currency is. While many people like to think of currency as the dollars and cents that they use to pay for things, it is much more than that. Currency is a *medium of exchange.* In other words, anything that you have that I agree can be exchanged for something that I have is a currency. If you have a Snickers bar and I have a Mars bar, yet you want the Mars bar, you can ask me if you can trade the Snickers for Mars. If I agree, then the Snickers has become the currency that you used to obtain the Mars.

This concept is very, very old; in fact, some archaeologists and anthropologists suggest that the use of currency is what defined the advent of human civilization. In ancient cultures, trading often occurred between people so that goods could be shared across the population. For example, a potter could trade his or her pottery with a farmer in exchange for food. In that case, the pottery became the currency, or the medium of exchange. Furthermore, people often traveled by land or sea to trade with other cultures. Whatever was agreed upon as a meaningful exchange became the currency used in the trade.

How was the value of currency determined? Well, largely by the individual people involved. If you wanted to buy clothes from me and pay for them using peacock feathers, but I had no use for peacock feathers, they would be worthless to me; therefore, I would not agree to the trade. However, if you wanted to pay for them in silver beads, and I knew that I could use those silver beads to buy something from somebody else, then that currency would have value to me. It would become the medium with which we would exchange our goods.

One feature of centralized governments is that the government became the regulating body of currency. In the United States, the dollar is minted by the US Treasury and, with some exceptions, is the only currency accepted as money. Currencies that are regulated by a central regulating body are known as fiat currencies. "Fiat" means "faith," and refers to the fact that use of the currency is not based on the intrinsic value of the paper used in the dollar (which is pretty close to worthless) but based on faith in the government that issued it. The government backs the currency and guarantees that it will not fail.

The value of the dollar is regulated by the government. It sets interest rates meant to raise or lower the dollar's value; therefore, however much money you may have in dollars, the value of that money is determined by the government.

This regulating concept is actually an abnormality in the basic laws of supply and demand, which define many modern economic theories. Usually, when something is in high demand, its value goes up because people become willing to pay more money for it. When something is in low demand, its value goes down because people aren't willing to pay as much for it. The value of the dollar (and many other fiat currencies, as well) is not determined by the demand for it but rather by what the government says its value is. In other words, the value of the dollar is artificial.

But what if there was a currency whose value was determined by popular demand? Think back to how currency used to function: simply as a medium of exchange that one party was willing to accept in return for its goods. Its value was determined by the people involved in the transaction, not by a centralized government that artificially determined what it was worth. That is the concept behind virtual currency, or cryptocurrency, as some call it.

Cryptocurrency is not regulated by any central government or regulating body; therefore, it is decentralized. Its value is not set by any individual but rather is determined by the people who use the currency, based on the laws of supply and demand.

This concept was behind the creation of Bitcoin, the first cryptocurrency. The creator, Satoshi Nakamoto, envisioned a currency that put power back into the hands of the people rather than fueling the government's own interests. Nearly ten years after Bitcoin's inception, even though the United States government has made many attempts to regulate it, it is still unregulated. Rather than being a liability, this lack of regulation has proven to be possibly Bitcoin's greatest asset. Popular demand of Bitcoin has skyrocketed, and in turn, so has its value. Its value has never been falsely inflated or deflated to reflect the caprices and whims of its governing body but rather is entirely linked to the demand that people have for it. Because of this, it is actually a truer currency than the dollar.

Vitalik Buterin, the creator of Ethereum, worked with the Bitcoin community for a few years before going rogue and creating his own blockchain. The idea of the Ether stems from that of Bitcoin, but with a crucial difference: While Bitcoin is not tied to any particular commodity, the Ether is. Ether is used to power the Ethereum network, so anyone who wants to use Ethereum must invest in Ether.

Like other cryptocurrencies, Ether does not exist in a physical form as cash. Rather, it is essentially a code. Ether has several different uses, which are outlined below.

Pay for gas. One use of Ether is to pay for gas, thereby enabling users to make a transaction on Ethereum. As previously explained, the amount of gas required to make a transaction is set, but the cost of the gas is determined by the user making the transaction. A sliding scale is shown, on which the user selects how much he or she wants to pay for gas. Paying more for gas makes that transaction a priority for the miners, who receive the fee as their compensation.

Invest. The value of the Ether has skyrocketed, going up 4500% just in the first half of 2017! This surge is due to increased use of the Ethereum network and therefore higher demand for the Ether. Major companies, such as JP Morgan and Merck, are beginning to experiment with Ethereum, meaning that they are also now making some exchanges in Ether.

In terms of investing, virtual currencies are far from a certain bet. They are historically known to be exceptionally volatile; now, with major investors joining the Ethereum market, there are concerns that the price could continue to surge before plummeting. Some individual projects that use Ether are now valued at hundreds of millions of dollars; if those projects should fail, they could potentially take the Ether market down with them.

Nevertheless, depending on your investment and other financial goals, Ether may prove to be a great use of your investment funds. When making any investment, but especially in cryptocurrency, the best rule of thumb is to only invest what you are willing to lose.

Chapter 4: Gas and Ether

In order to invest in Ether, you will need to get a virtual currency wallet. A wallet functions much the same as your bank account's online service; you log in to your account and see a ledger of your transaction history.

There are several different types of wallets, and whichever one you choose should be the one that will best help you meet your goals. All types of virtual currency wallets are classified as either hot or cold. A hot wallet is one that operates online, meaning that it is always connected to the Internet. These wallets are the easiest for hackers to access, so storing large amounts of cryptocurrency in them is not recommended. Hot wallets are best suited for people who engage in frequent trading and therefore need ongoing access to their wallets. A cold wallet is one that operates offline on the user's computer desktop; the only way for hackers to access it is for them to first access the desktop. Cold storage is best for long-term investing and holding larger amounts of cryptocurrency.

Coinbase is the most popular wallet for buying and trading Ether. Make sure that the wallet you choose trades in Ether. Usually, you can buy Ether directly from the wallet. You purchase the Ether using fiat currency — usually dollars, but other currencies, such as pounds and Euros, may be accepted as well — based on the current exchange rate. For example, if the current value of Ether is $400, then you will pay $400 to purchase one Ether. You can also purchase portions of an Ether by choosing to pay a set amount of fiat currency in exchange for the same value of Ether.

How Does Ether Work?

New Ether are created through the process of mining. Every time a miner solves the mathematical problem associated with a block of transactions, five new Ether are created and rewarded to that miner. If another miner simultaneously finds a solution to the same block of transactions, he or she may be rewarded with two or three Ether (referred to as the aunt/uncle reward).

The Ether holds a crucial place in the Ethereum economy. Without it, the network would be unable to run because it fuels the apps and transactions that the network processes.

As a cryptocurrency, its uses outside of Ethereum are limited. Bitcoin can be used to buy and sell everyday goods, such as a cup of coffee or a bag of groceries. It is accepted by many large retailers, such as overstock.com and Microsoft, as well as a growing number of small businesses. It can even be used at some universities to pay for tuition! Ether, however, does not currently have those same uses. It is not accepted by retailers the way that Bitcoin is. This presents another crucial difference between Bitcoin and the Ether, or rather the mirror image of the fact that Bitcoin is not connected to any commodity while the Ether is. Bitcoin hit the mainstream partially because of its appeal as an alternative way to pay for everyday goods; if it couldn't be used by average people in their daily lives, it would have remained a fringe interest of the technophile community. The Ether was created for the simple (although not entirely exclusive) purpose of fueling the Ethereum network. Users must invest in the Ether and use it to pay for the transactions that they make. Therefore, its value is tied to how many people are using the Ethereum network.

The growing number of people using Ethereum, combined with the sheer amount of money being invested by these people (and now large companies) in Ethereum projects is causing the value of the Ether to skyrocket. While the values of both Bitcoin and the Ether are connected to the laws of supply and demand, they operate for different purposes.

Think of Bitcoin as gold and the Ether as a diamond. Gold is a medium of exchange but has few purposes beyond that. It has no real industrial use, but its value tends to be quite high because people are willing to pay a lot of money for it. Gold jewelry is worth a lot because a lot of people want it; therefore, their higher demand attributes a higher value to it. Diamonds, on the other hand, are worth a lot on their own merit as a medium of exchange, but also have industrial use. They aren't only used in expensive jewelry, whose value is given to it based solely on how much people are willing to pay for it. They are also used in things such as saws and in procedures such as cutting, grinding, and polishing. Nothing is harder than a diamond, so diamonds have great use outside of being a medium of exchange.

Like gold, Bitcoin is not connected to a commodity. Its value is not based on any particular commodity but rather on how much people are willing to pay for it. The Ether, like a diamond, is worth a lot of money as a medium of exchange (it has grown in value over 4500% just in the first half of 2017), but it is more than that. It is what connects people to the Ethereum network and allows them to use it.

Chapter 5:
Applications on Ethereum

As previously explained, Ethereum powers a new kind of app, a decentralized application, referred to as a Dapp. This chapter will look at some of the Dapps that run on Ethereum, with the intent of giving you an idea of what kind of application is best suited to this platform.

Gnosis

Gnosis is a platform for making market predictions based on the consensus of a large group of people. This is referred to as crowd-sourced wisdom. For example, imagine that you ask a random person on the street who he thinks will win tonight's football game between the Horses and the Donkeys. That random person might not even know that there is a football game, and probably won't even care. However, if you got together hundreds or even thousands of people who are interested in football and are fans of one of the teams involved, the situation will be entirely different. Some of those fans may know their team's stats up and down the board and be able to accurately predict how well one team will fare (or not fare) against the other. With the wisdom of all those people combined, the odds of a successful prediction are significantly higher.

This principle of crowd-sourced wisdom is the idea behind Gnosis. Anyone can create an event, say, who will win the football game. Users of Gnosis can use their Gnosis tokens (whose value is set against the Ether) to make bets based on what they believe the outcome will be. The users who correctly predicted the outcome will divide the earnings between themselves.

Other than making money, the idea is to enable people to know in advance what will probably happen in the future, whether that be clear skies tomorrow or the stock market crashing.

FirstBlood

FirstBlood is what happens when the world of e-sports is connected to the power of a blockchain. Traditionally, the e-sports community is subject to a lot of regulation and corruption by the middlemen supposedly performing said regulation. There is also a lot of downtime, hacking, and problems with money transfers. FirstBlood aims to revolutionize e-sports by doing away with all of those problems.

Because of the secure blockchain network on which it operates. FirstBlood is not prone to hacking or any other security problems. Instead of betting with fiat currency through any traditional middleman, such as PayPal, bets are made in the token 1ST, the virtual currency of FirstBlood. The money is held in a smart contract until the winner of a match is declared. The money is then awarded to those who bet on the winner.

To make sure that the winner is reported accurately, FirstBlood randomly selects Witnesses from computer nodes on the network. The Witnesses are required to declare the winner and are compensated for their work. In order to become a Witness, individuals must submit a smart contract with a certain amount of 1ST tokens.

In the event of a disputed match, a Jury is selected from among those who watched the match. The Jurors report on who won the match and are compensated for their work. However, those who reported against what the majority determined may actually be penalized for false reporting.

Via FirstBlood, e-sports is becoming more transparent and free from the corruption that plagues the traditional industry.

Alice.SI

When deciding to donate to a charity, individuals are faced with the daunting task of determining whether or not a charity is legitimate. In the wake of catastrophes, such as Hurricane Katrina or the 2004 tsunami in Southeast Asia, false charities pop up to take advantage of the people who are ready and willing to give to those who are in desperate need. Now, with crowd-funding sites such as GoFundMe and Kickstarter, the problem is occurring at an even more grassroots level. Fraud on these websites runs rampant and is largely unchecked, so people end up inadvertently donating money to "causes" that are actually hoaxes. Some feel that this kind of fraud — taking money from kind-hearted people who are trying to give to those who are in need — has caused them to lose faith in humanity.

Ethereum

Enter Alice.SI. This Dapp was designed to provide accountability to charities by ensuring that they actually perform the work that they claim to do. When users want to donate to a charity but want to first confirm that it is legitimate, they can create a smart contract on Alice.SI, which will hold their funds until the charity in question proves that it has, in fact, done the work that it promised.

As you can probably see, applications on Ethereum are about engaging people as communities, which is reflective of the peer-to-peer structure of blockchain. People come together on these applications to engage in meaningful transactions with total transparency and without fear of corruption.

Chapter 6:
How to use Ethereum to Build an Application

This chapter will not get into all of the background knowledge required behind how to build an application, such as writing computer code or envisioning a concept for an app. It will rather give you an overview of the process involved in creating an application on Ethereum, which is different than creating apps on other platforms.

Before you can begin to turn your great idea into a Dapp, you need to become more familiar with the Ethereum network. You will probably want to look around at some Dapps to see what they do and how they work, to help you get an idea of what you want your Dapp to look like and how it should function. You will also want to look at different ways that people raised money for their Dapps, such as initial coin offerings (ICO's) and crowd-funding. You will also want to become a part of the blockchain community by joining chat rooms, blogs, and other forms of communication commonly used by those on blockchain. Making connections will not only help you raise money to fund your Dapp but will also put you in a better position for getting answers to the questions that will undoubtedly arise in the process of Dapp creation.

Will your Dapp be a type 1, type 2, or type 3? Remember that a type 1 is an entirely new blockchain, such as Bitcoin or Ethereum. That is probably too ambitious for your first Dapp, so you will want to make it either a type 2 or type 3. Type 2 Dapps are written onto the main blockchain, and Type 3 Dapps are built onto other pre-existing Dapps. Whichever one you decide will affect every step of the process.

Next, you will need to decide which programming language to use. Talk to people in the blockchain community to decide which programming language will be best. If you are more knowledgeable about one particular programming language, that will probably be the one that you will decide to use. However, there may be another programming language that is more suited to your Dapp. If that is the case, you will either need to become proficient in that programming language or hire someone who is. Keep in mind that one of the incentives behind the use of gas on Ethereum is to make the Dapps as efficient as possible. Inefficient, wasteful code costs more to execute, so while using a different programming language than what you are accustomed to may be difficult in the short-run, it will produce long-term benefits.

Then, you will need to decide on a framework to use. A framework supports the development of the application. Solidity, which was created for Ethereum, has two frameworks: Truffle and Embark. Truffle is the most popular framework. It a built-in compilation of smart contracts, which will be one of the central features of your Dapp. Embark allows for decentralized storage and decentralized communication; whether you choose to use Truffle or Embark will be based on your goals for your Dapp. Again, discussing which one will be best with members of the blockchain community will be in your best interest. You'll be talking with people who have already gone through this process and have the bruises to prove it. They will be able to share with you the wisdom they gained from their successes and failures. You will need to download and install the framework that you wish to use.

You will need to use the Ethereum home page (www.ethereum.org) to create a virtual currency on which your Dapp will run. The value of this virtual currency will be against the Ether (as opposed to the dollar or any other fiat or virtual currency) and will go up or down based on how successful your Dapp is. If you wish to hold an ICO to help raise money for the creation of your Dapp, you will need to have a strong proposal for what the Dapp will do and how it will work. Share this proposal with the blockchain community and see how much support you are able to get. You may have to invest some of your own money, but that doesn't mean your Dapp won't be successful.

Next is the intensive, time-consuming process of writing the code that will create and execute the Dapp. The code is incredibly important; anyone on the blockchain will be able to see it. The one heist that happened on Ethereum — that of the DAO in June of 2016 — happened hours after the Dapp was created because someone found a weakness in the code, which he exploited to siphon off tens of millions of dollars' worth of Ether. Because blockchain transactions are tamper-proof, the code cannot be changed. This means that if someone was to find a weakness in your code, you would only be able to sit back and helplessly watch all of the funds be depleted from your Dapp.

If you want to charge a transaction fee, that will probably need to be written into the initial code. Any other features, especially those generating income, will also need to be in the initial code, as the code cannot be changed.

Once the code is written, you will need to test out your Dapp in a sandbox. Using a sandbox will prevent the entire system from being affected should there be an error in your code. If you find any kind of weakness in it, you will be able to fix it without any financial or reputational repercussions (and in the world of Ethereum, reputational repercussions can be far worse than financial ones). Once you are satisfied with the code, have some technophile friends test it out. See if they are able to find a weakness in it that would be exploitable by someone on the blockchain.

Once your code is set and the Dapp is executable, it's time to launch it. Congratulations for achieving this milestone, and best of luck.

Chapter 7:
How to Make Money with Ethereum

Create a Dapp

One way to make money with Ethereum is to create your own Dapp. While the mechanics of how to create a Dapp involves the use of advanced computer coding, which is far beyond the scope of this ebook, this section will explain how a Dapp can generate income.

While your Dapp is in the process of being created (from your conception of the idea until it is released), you can generate money via a crowd sale. Ethereum has options for you to create your own virtual currency as part of your Dapp; you can hold an initial coin offering (ICO) in which people can invest in your virtual currency and, by extension, your Dapp. You can also launch a campaign on a site such as GoFundMe or Kickstarter to help fund your Dapp. The blockchain community tends to be extremely supportive, and some people have made millions of dollars off of it. They tend to want to help other people succeed, as well. Get your idea out to the community. Let people know that you are fully intent on making it work and that you have the competencies and resources (including time) required. And then see where that will take you.

Ethereum

Another way to make money via Ethereum Dapps is to charge a transaction fee. While in an ideal world we would be able to pursue our passions without having to worry about money, we live in a world in which money is essential to survival. Before you decide to charge a fee, you need to keep in mind two things. The first is that because Ethereum is an open-source blockchain, the information on it is not owned by anybody. Meaning that the information on your Dapp is not owned by you. The second thing to remember is that blockchain was created to put power back into the hands of the populace rather than in the hands of wealthy CEOs and the one percent. Don't become of the mindset that you will become like a wealthy CEO, or you will quickly lose the support of the blockchain community. Make your fees reasonable and as low as possible while still generating income for yourself. Because Ethereum Dapps run on smart contracts, every time a contract is made, the user sends a fee in Ether. You can opt to receive a cut of that fee.

A convenient way for both you and your users to make money off of your Dapp is to put ads on your Dapp. You will need to get businesses to agree to advertise on your Dapp for a certain amount of money each time the ad is viewed. Nobody likes having to watch ads (think of when a YouTube video gets interrupted by one), but what if your users could get paid for watching the ads on your Dapp? Give your users a share of the money generated from the ad and keep the rest for yourself. This feature alone could attract multiple new users to your Dapp, thereby increasing your income base.

There are other standard profit-generating strategies that have been used by traditional apps for years. They include charging a membership fee, charging a download fee, and paying for the services provided. One method that has been particularly successful is giving some basic version of the app for free; once users decide that they like it, they can pay to download the full version. All of the traditional methods for generating money on apps can be transferred to Dapps.

If coding is beyond your capabilities and interest, don't worry. There are still other ways that you can make money on Ethereum.

Mine on Ethereum

Becoming a miner on Ethereum is another way to generate income, as miners are rewarded with five Ether for each mathematical problem that they correctly solve. If the value of the Ether is at $300, then solving one of those problems will net you $1500! That is one way to pay off student loans.

There are two things that you will need in order to mine in such a way as to actually generate money. The first is an alternative energy source, such as solar or wind, to power your computer. Keep in mind that running a blockchain is extremely energy-intensive, and a lot of that energy is consumed from the process of mining. Using regular fossil fuel-powered electricity can actually make the mining process unprofitable because of how much you will pay in electricity costs.

The second thing that you will need is a computer outfitted with a graphics processing unit, or GPU, as even the most basic models of these run up to 200 times faster than a standard PC outfitted with a traditional CPU processor. A CPU processor is so inefficient that attempting to mine with it will be unprofitable.

Most mining computers are Windows-based, so the following guidelines are applicable to Windows. If you set up a Mac as a mining computer, you will probably need to tweak this information somewhat. You won't need to download the entire Ethereum blockchain onto your mining computer, which is great because it is over 20 gigabytes and growing! You will need to download a client, the mining app, and the Ethereum wallet.

Downloading the client will turn your computer into an Ethereum node and connect it to every other node on the Ethereum network. There are numerous clients that you can use; the most popular one, geth, runs on the command-line script Go. You will need to do some research to figure out which client is best suited for your knowledge base. In addition to connecting you to the Ethereum network as a node computer, the client will enable you to write smart contracts.

You will also need an Ethereum Mist wallet. You can easily find the wallet by searching online. It will download as a zip file; you will need to unzip and run it. Then, you will need to create an account so that you can send and receive Ether.

Next, you will need to download the mining app, Ethminer. Once Ethminer is installed, your computer will become part of the network that secures the Ethereum blockchain. You will also be able to begin mining.

There are two ways to mine. The first way is to go solo. Going solo means that you will have much less chance of solving the cryptographic puzzles necessary to win Ether, but whenever you do, you will get the entire payout. The other way is to join a mining pool. Mining pools combine the computational power of all of the users and split the payout equitably depending on how much power each user contributed. Miners who join mining pools tend to make more money, even though the payout on each solution is lower, because they are a part of so many more solutions. The number of members and amount of computational power that each mining pool has is constantly changing, so if you do join a mining pool, try to stay up to speed on the pool's stats.

Invest in the Ether

Another way to make money on Ethereum is to invest in the Ether. Cryptocurrencies are like traditional investments in many ways. You pay a dollar amount for the share (or in this case, the amount of Ether) that you want to buy. If the company (in this case, the Ethereum network) grows, then the value of the share, or Ether, grows, as well. Watch it grow your investment holdings.

There is one important distinction between investing in Ether and in traditional shares of a company: the rate at which the investment grows. Traditional investments may grow at a rate of two to three percent a year; growth of ten percent is considered rather high. The value of the Ether has grown by 4500 percent just in the first half of 2017! What that means for investors is if that rate of growth continues, instead of their money growing by maybe a paltry ten percent per year, it could grow by nearly 10,000 percent! There really is no easier way to make money.

Typically, high-yield investments are seen as risky; this principle is also true of cryptocurrency. Historically, cryptocurrencies have been subject to extreme volatility. The early years of Bitcoin saw periods in which its value would double in a matter of weeks, sometimes only in days, followed by a crash in which the currency would lose most of its value. Crashes were usually induced by massive thefts (like the infamous Mt. Gox heist that ultimately cost trillions of dollars and wiped out the holdings of thousands of Bitcoin investors). However, security protocols for wallets that hold cryptocurrencies have increased tremendously, making security breaches a much more unusual phenomenon.

The major volatility of the Bitcoin market was also tied to the fact that, in its early days, not a lot of people used Bitcoin. Imagine a cannonball being dropped into a puddle of water. The entire system of water will be disrupted by the weight of the cannonball, simply because there is not much water present. However, if the same cannonball was dropped into an Olympic-sized swimming pool, it would create a relatively small splash, compared to the overall size of the pool. It might generate some small waves, but it wouldn't prove catastrophic to the pool the way that it would to the puddle. In the early days of Bitcoin when far fewer people were using the cryptocurrency, a theft was the equivalent of a cannonball being dropped into a puddle. Some, such as the Mt. Gox heist, proved to be nearly fatal to the entire Bitcoin community and nearly ended the run of virtual currency. However, now the Bitcoin community is so large that a large theft would be more like dropping a cannonball into an Olympic-sized swimming pool. Its effects would certainly be felt, but it wouldn't devastate the economy.

Ethereum has so many users who hold Ether that it is like the Olympic-sized swimming pool. In other words, even if a massive heist occurred, the felt impact would actually be quite small. There was a major crash that happened in the summer of 2017, following a rumor that Vitalik Buterin had died. The value of the Ether plummeted from approximately $300 to only about ten cents. However, it quickly regained its value and continued its upward trend of growth. All that is to say that while cryptocurrencies have historically been incredibly volatile, those wild swings are not nearly as wild or as frequent today.

Because the Ether is tied to a commodity — Ethereum — which is becoming increasingly popular and gaining traction even with multinational companies such as JPMorgan, demand for it, and with it its value, will probably continue to rise for the foreseeable future.

However, there is always a possibility that what some consider to be "the cryptocurrency experiment" will fail, causing investors to lose all of their holdings. A good rule of thumb is to only invest what you are willing to lose. Extra cash earned from a side gig, money that you saved by cooking at home instead of going out to eat, and a Christmas bonus from work are all good forms of income for investing in cryptocurrency. You probably won't starve or lose all of your retirement savings if the $50 that you earned mowing yards or shoveling snow went into the Ether before it crashed. You should not invest your retirement fund, your kid's college fund, or the money that you have saved for a down payment on a house in Ether or any cryptocurrency. If the market crashes, you will lose all of your holdings. Cryptocurrencies have consistently defied all of the dire predictions that economists have made, but this does not mean that they are invulnerable.

Another important investment decision is to diversify your portfolio, just like you would with a traditional investment. If you decide to invest in cryptocurrencies, invest in the Ether and in some other cryptocurrency, such as the LSK (which is connected to Lisk), Bitcoin, or LiteCoin. That way, if one currency should fail, you won't lose all of your holdings.

Conclusion

In conclusion, the potential that Ethereum has is limited only by the interests, talents, and capacities of the people who use it. As an open-source blockchain, none of the information on it is owned by any one person — not even its creator — but rather is shared by everyone on the network. This method of distributing information ensures that no one person is able to wield an incongruent amount of power or have leverage over others, which presents a drastic paradigm shift from the traditional concept of having a centralized governing body.

Vitalik Buterin envisioned that blockchain could be used for more than supporting the Bitcoin network, and his creation of Ethereum proved that this was true. Because of Ethereum, more and more people are able to access the benefits of blockchain, such as its transparent and trustless nature. One might even say that while Bitcoin created blockchain, Ethereum revolutionized it.

There are several ways that anyone with a computer and a little bit of know-how can generate income from Ethereum. One way is to create a Dapp and use any of the income-generating methods described in the last chapter. Another way is to mine for Ether, the virtual currency used to power the

Ethereum

Ethereum network, and yet another way is to invest in Ether, as its value has soared exponentially.

Whatever you decide to do with Ethereum is entirely up to you. You may find that you are able to generate a steady stream of passive income, or maybe even find that you are its next overnight success story. The possibilities are limitless.

Finally, if you found this book useful in any way, a review on Amazon is always appreciated!

Lightning Source UK Ltd.
Milton Keynes UK
UKHW040243070821
388264UK00003B/8